DEC - 9 2009

DATE DUE

Fearsome Fascinations

Edited & Designed by Whitney Scott

Outrider Press, Inc.

Fearsome Fascinations is published by Outrider Press in affiliation with TallGrass Writers Guild.

Trademarks and brand names have been printed in initial capital letters

Book Design & Production by Whitney Scott

Amanda Caverzasi's "The Jameson's Bash" appeared in *Bad Idea*.

Jan Chronister's "Radium Girl" first appeared in *Target Practice*

"Voices in the Fire" by Lynn Veach Sadler first appeared in *Penny Dreadful*.

Noel Sloboda's "How It Goes Down" originally appeared in *Right Hand Pointing*.

Lynn Tait's "Eden's Bar & Grill" was previously published in *Re:al* (U.S).

Marilyn Taylor's "The Showdown" originally appeared in *Shadows Like These*, Wm. Caxton Ltd. Ms. Taylor's "Studying the Menu" first appeared in *The Alabama Literary Review*.

© 2009, Outrider Press, Inc.
ISBN 09712903-6-9

Outrider Press, Inc.
2036 Northwinds Drive
Dyer IN 46311

Publication made possible in part by a grant from the Illinois Arts Council

for all who write despite their fears

Contents

Poetry

1st Prize–Ann McGovern
"How Do You Cook...?"

2nd Place–Claudia Van Gerven
"Once Touched by the Wolf"

3rd Place–Marilyn Taylor
"The Showdown"

Hon. Mention–Anthony White
"Spider Silk is Stronger..."

Prose

1st Prize–Vincenzo Benestante
"The Boy Who Loved..."

2nd Place–James Wall
"The Town That Ate the Chef"

3rd Place–Lones Seiber
"Fields Where Glory..."

Hon. Mention–Eve Edelson
"The Underachiever"

⋮

10

⋮

The Universal Parade

Bret Angelos

Paris wanted some pasta. Correction. Paris needed pasta. Her five o'clock bar hangover was killing her, she'd slept through breakfast and brunch, and was pushing the limits on lunch at 3 P.M. Advil and a brief shower motivated her as she limped over to the Double D for cheap consumables—accent on cheap considering last night's massive bar tab and her lack of a real job.

Double D Liquors was the right place for this economical repast. The usual burnouts ogled her on the way into the store.

"I got my eye on you baby! Give me some more shake and bake, hot stuff!" a tall, balding man in skintight jeans and an extra large wool overcoat said as he stiffly focused his imaginary telescope on Paris's caboose.

His Mexican compadre nodded, adding, "Spare some change, baby. Reach into that goldmine of a back pocket and make a bum's day."

Paris nonchalantly flipped them the finger and proceeded inside.

The Arab owner recognized her and waved. "Hello, hello. We've got a great deal on Old Style today. The cheapest price in the city! Nobody beats my price on a 15-pack of Old Style. You like the Old Style, no?"

"Not today. I'm hangin' pretty hard and I need chow. Booze later."

She made her way past stacks of beer and cases of wine to the dry goods aisle, which appeared practically untouched. A fine layer of dust covered an assortment of Campbell's soup, Ramen noodles, Hormel chili, and Ritz crackers. A set of finger prints marked a package of Fig Newtons. A crime scene investigator or an archeologist couldn't have asked for a better find.

Paris leaned over and examined her pasta options. It was Wednesday and she had five bucks left till the weekend and needed to make the most of it. Her right index finger ticked down the stacks of pasta leaving a trail of clear packaging and a wake of dust. The magic finger finally settled on Parade Brand pasta. There was no beating the 69-cent price. Paris picked up a box of Parade Brand pasta and inspected it. The sell-by date was past due and for all she knew this box had been there for years. Obviously Parade Brand pasta was an extremely shelf stable product. Paris knew a food chemist and she always got a kick out of the term "shelf stable." Apparently Cheese Whiz was the king of shelf stability. Keep a gross of Cheese Whiz in the bomb shelter and the nuclear winter would be a breeze.

She held up the box of Parade Brand pasta triumphantly and joked to herself and the Arab store owner peeping at her in the convex mirror, "It's pasta for all my friends!"

Paris didn't know it, but she had inadvertently kicked off an elaborate and quite elegant sub-atomic process in Double D Liquors. As she grabbed a couple more boxes of pasta, the chain reaction had already begun. The limits of shelf stability had been reached and the conditions were ripe for a reversal. The Holy Grail of any food chemist's career was a singular moment discussed in hushed tones at cocktail parties and imagined at Twinkie factories everywhere. This critical moment was known as "shelf instability"—the precise second when previously rock-solid structures composing the food item begin to pancake down on one and other. Ultimately the enormous pressures and energies released by this breakdown result in the collapse of the product into a single point in space. The dry goods aisle of Double D Liquors would prove to be the site of this curious spatial anomaly.

Paris was still laughing to herself when she noticed the shudder. The temperature in the aisle shot up instantly and a wave of pressure pushed her towards a stack of Old Style. As she was about to crash into the cheapest Old Style in the city, she felt the push turn into a pull and she was yo-yoed back towards the pasta shelf. Time slowed, becoming irrelevant. Puzzled, Paris looked toward the door and could see herself entering the store while simultaneously watching herself pick up that first package of Parade Brand pasta in triumph.

The scene shifted, and the aisle was twisted and warped almost beyond recognition, its contents fused into a giant smoldering ball. A fire marshal and a police captain looked on as evidence technicians prepared to sift through the wreckage.

"It's one hell of a way to go out," the fireman said, trying to pry a can of sardines away from the mass of metal that was the dry goods shelf.

The police captain answered grimly, "Yeah. Those two bums out front saw the flash and she was gone. Normally I'd say bring the bomb squad on this one, but I've never seen anything like it."

The fireman added, "The owner watched her pick up some spaghetti and then boom—gone! It's not every day your usual spaghetti recipe turns into some kind of super-string theory implosion."

Surprised at the fireman's know-how, the captain said, "Who am I talking to? Stephen fucking Hawkings? Where's this shit coming from?"

"PBS." The fire marshal was interrupted by one of the evidence techs. "I think we've got something over here, sir."

Paris had blacked out. Slowly she regained consciousness, heard a man talking to himself, and opened her eyes, but could only make out shadows. She was lying flat on her back, with someone hovering over her.

"Almost got it. There we go. She's all set. I think she's awake."

Her vision came into focus on a pale-faced man with bright red hair, a baton, and a blue cape leaning down. He came closer. "Good day, Miss. How are you feeling?"

Paris felt amazingly good. Her hangover was gone and she felt like she had slept for a week. She sat up and realized that she was no longer in Double D Liquors. Closer inspection revealed that she was no longer in Chicago. In fact, Paris was lying on an enormous, flat green lawn that extended in all directions. The sky, a mix of reds, pinks and blues had a trace of white clouds to round out the cartoon-ish color palette of this bizarre place.

A tingle of suspicion crept up her neck as Paris rubbed her eyes, saying, "Where the hell am I?"

He put his hand on her shoulder. "I know this must be a shock to you, Miss. My name is Franz. On behalf of Grand Marshal Enzo Marconi, I would like to welcome you to the Universal Parade. As the newest arrival, you'll be the guest of honor at the Parade. I've taken the liberty of applying some special contacts to your eyes. They will allow you to enjoy the Parade more completely."

Guest of honor, Paris thought. Doesn't sound good. An image formed in her mind, maybe from too much *Gilligan's Island* as a child. She was in a large black cauldron. People were tossing in carrots and other veggies into the broth. Smack in the middle of this island stew— Paris—the guest of honor and soup d'jour.

"This is really whacked, Franz! A second ago I was picking up pasta in the Double D. Now you're saying I'm the special guest at some goddamn parade. What's the deal?"

"I realize this is confusing, Paris. You have been transported to the Universal Parade through a wormhole from your world." He paused, considering. "It's not entirely possible to explain how you've come to the Universal Parade or where in fact the Universal Parade is. The details are really..." he trailed off, then continued with a new briskness, "Suffice it to say that you are now in a place beyond the normal four dimensions that you know and love. Considering the fact that there are anywhere between seven and twenty-three dimensions curled up in the normal four, you could be anywhere, but the most important fact to remember is that you're here, and you're the guest of honor at the Universal Parade."

This brightly colored lunatic knew her name and seemed to think she was the guest of honor at an unknown parade in an unknown land. He'd had put an unknown substance into her eyes and done lord knows what to her while she was out. Fear rose from the pit of her stomach, washed over her chest and threatened to suffocate her. She tried to scream, but was unable to let it out. No air could get into her lungs.

Urban defense mechanisms hard wired into her lower brainstem took control. Chicago toughness, gained from years of life on the edge, spoke up: half defiant, half smartass. "OK, Franz. I can dig that. I've watched the *Twilight Zone*. But how the hell do you know my name? Is everyone psychic at the Universal Parade?"

Franz pulled Paris to her feet. "No, Miss. I went through your pockets. Many apologies. Now it's time for the Parade, and you choose whatever pleases you."

They walked a circuitous path worn into the enormous green lawn. Nothing appeared on the horizon in any direction. Startled, Paris realized the lawn existed solely for them both, and she proceeded cautiously.

Franz was in front continuing his lecture on Universal Parade basics. "You may be wondering, what in God's name did I put in your eyes?"

Bravado overcame fear. "Actually Franz, I really dig these contacts. I see a lot better."

"An added benefit. They give the wearer perfect vision. Everyone has eagle eyes at the Universal Parade. I should mention that the contacts are permanent. They adhere to the surface of the eye with self applying micro-sutures. They are also capable of receiving massive amounts of high band width."

Paris gave a confused shrug, "Meaning?"

"High definition digital images can be beamed wirelessly into your eyes."

Her eyes narrowed in suspicion. "For the purpose of?"

Franz explained, "We have developed a parade that can be

enjoyed by all people, no matter what their preference, simultaneously. This is the reason for the Universal Parade. It occurs all the time and, with the assistance of those special contacts, can take any form you wish. You simply tell the baton twirler what you want and we make it happen."

"So...parades, huh—what's the big deal?"

Franz stopped, gazing at her with great reverence, "It's the will of the Great String."

"This Great String's your god?"

Franz pulled out his baton, "It's what connects everything everywhere together. We go where it pleases and exist because of it. It is beyond forces. It takes no heed of nuclear forces or gravity because it created them. The Great String is the reason that you and countless beings are in this place. Look around the grandstand, Paris. The Universal Parade is truly universal."

Paris looked and saw a long grandstand extending to the horizon. Her eagle eye contacts kicked in and she saw that the crowd was not all human. Beings of almost every imaginable type sat together calmly awaiting the Universal Parade.

Franz twirled a baton expertly while waiting for Paris's parade choices. She went with St. Patrick's Day, the Fourth of July, and a little Gay Pride. The crowd began to buzz with activity and the kind of energy a child might feel right before a parade. A procession of people in bright green body suits passed before the grandstand.

"Franz, what's with the body suits?"

"Those are the Neutrals. They create the Universal Parade. We project the parade images onto them. It is a great honor to be among their number."

"These Neutrals wear green. So it's like a green screen that we use for our weather reports?"

Franz tossed his baton high in the air and answered as he caught it without looking, "No Paris, we could project the images onto anything. We just like green."

What followed could only be described as many simultaneous moments of pure joy. The column of Neutrals marched in front of the grandstand in an endless procession that appeared to alternate between Paris's preferences. The entire grandstand was cheering as millions of different parades occurred simultaneously. Paris couldn't know how long the Universal Parade had been going. There was too much pleasure being taken from all of parties involved to keep track of time.

Paris tried to get Franz's attention. "What are you watching?"

He was enjoying his own private parade which took place in 23 dimensions, and couldn't be described at a level she could possibly understand. "It's quite a spectacle, Paris. You'd like it very much."

"Awesome! I love the Universal Parade!"

"It is hoped by all that we may one day share the Universal Parade with everyone. All who come here are forever connected to us. The Great String will one day make true our most dearly held maxim." He smiled. "The Universe loves a parade."

When it was over, Paris was exhausted, yet exhilarated, her former fears forgotten. "Franz, I'm pooped—but when is the next parade?"

"Right now if you want."

She shook her head. "I need a break. I haven't strengthened my parade lungs like the rest of you. And I'm getting a little light headed..." Her voice trailed off as the shudder returned; the cosmic yo-yo started up again, and in an instant Paris was gone.

She woke up back in the Double D under a pile of Old Style, realizing the Universal Parade was no more. Franz and the Parade were coiled up somewhere in another dimension. She felt sad at having missed the next parade as real life concerns came back into focus with money, food, and rent taking priority. Reality in four dimensions was a real bear.

An EMT examined her. "Looks like something's in your eyes. Do you wear contacts?"

In the distance, two blocks away, she spotted the homeless man and his Mexican friend talking to each other. Paris could read their lips from two blocks away. Suddenly the man's wool overcoat turned into a green and white t-shirt that said "Kiss me, I'm Irish," and his Mexican compadre's Cubs shirt switched over to a rainbow that read "Alive with Pride."

"Yes, I wear contacts," she said, smiling. "I just got a new pair."

A twenty-three dimensional string had uncoiled. It was finer than the finest angel hair pasta, and this super-spaghetti strand now pulsed with the happy bandwidth of the Universal Parade.

Bad Boy Love
Pattie Baker

Not preposterous,
The rhinoceros but marvelous
and not to be messed with.
This Sherman tank of the jungle
can pull rank on any among us.
Hide almost impenetrable,
stumpy legs faster than possible,
and oh those horns
sharper than Einstein's musings
Imagine a rhino's shock
When a rifle takes him out
In order to grind to powder
That elegant horn's power
Which, by the way, is untransferable.

⋮

18

⋮

The Boy Who Loved Horror Stories

Vincenzo Benestante

Fairly early in life, Julian began to devour all the horror stories he could lay his hands on. They were his passion and solace. He enjoyed science fiction as well, but horror, ah, *horror*! The other children never harassed Julian, but they never paid much attention to him, either. He was short, slightly overweight and wore glasses. They weren't too thick, but together with his phenotype and broad mouth, they accentuated his striking resemblance to a frog. Nonetheless, Julian was aware of the fact that he was reasonably lucky. At least he was not a target for every bully in the neighborhood. Even these boys ignored him largely—no doubt sensing that he'd probably not be worth the trouble. Julian had to admit to himself that he looked like somebody who'd start to bawl and scream before anyone even laid a hand on him.

But whatever the reason, they left him alone. Everybody left him alone. Julian was a very good pupil, yet not so ostensible as to earn the reputation of being a brownnose. He would have liked to have played with other children now and then, but he was neither sufficiently fast, nor skillful enough to be able to compete in their games or sports. His classmates, on the other hand, were not interested in the adventure episodes Julian invented. They possessed neither the imagination, nor the ability to concentrate intensely enough for improvisation and role-playing. Julian had therefore no recourse but to live alone in his domain of fantasy. The books helped. He could slip into the role of the protagonist of a story so easily and completely that he almost forgot he was lying down in his room, reading.

At age ten—after he had discovered H.P. Lovecraft—there was no holding him back: the boy spent every free moment engrossed in tales and novels of the supernatural and unholy. In this world of insanity and terror, he found an escape from his dreary existence. Aside from the frightful insanity of Lovecraft, he also lost himself in the subtle, whispered horrors of Ambrose Bierce. Bram Stoker gave him access to the restless, melancholy wisdom of the undead. He was grateful to Henry James for two sleepless nights of delicious shivering at every breeze, recognizing that the wind carried the painful moaning of those who had died with hate and greed coloring their final thoughts.

Not only the old masters filled his life with awe and wonder over the secrets of the ancient and nearly immortal evil of the universe. The contemporary greats of the supernatural and fantastic genre enriched Julian's mind with understanding for the agony of the power unattainable to mortals: James Herbert, Clive Barker and above all, nearly god-like in his power to teach even the most hardened of men to fear their very shadows: Stephen King. The boy lived nowhere with such intensity as in these grand, epic journeys into the unfathomable human soul.

But that wasn't all. With awakening puberty, Julian made an astounding discovery. One night he experienced his first nocturnal emission. But this was not the result of a dream of sexual play with a beautiful, naked girl.

Julian was quite disturbed upon awakening the following morning: not about the orgasm; he had known about that, knew it was a physical sign of natural, hormonal development. No, it was the cause of this first erotic experience which confused him: during the night, Julian had dreamed he was running over an open field. At first disoriented, because the dream simply began with Julian's running, he thought he was perhaps fleeing. But after only a few moments, he noticed two unusual facts: first of all, he was not the least bit fatigued from running. In fact, his body seemed to rejoice in it. Secondly, he was naked. It must have been a warm summer evening in the dream, because the meadow was a full and brilliant green. The longer Julian ran, the more ... sensual the physical experience grew. As he immersed himself deeper and deeper into the pleasure of running, a shrill sound —which he first interpreted as the screeching of a bird—forced itself into his awareness.

But it was only his alarm clock and he sat up abruptly to silence it. That was when he discovered the dampness in his lap. He remembered a moment of ecstasy—shortly before the alarm went off —during which the semen had shot forth in hot, rhythmic and lustful eruptions. He remained sitting in bed for a few minutes, in order to recapture and hold all the elements of the dream. It was the most vivid dream he had ever experienced: an almost magical occurrence, similar to the entrance into another dimension, as described so palpably by August Derleth. Or like the strange, visionary narratives between the episodes in

Ray Bradbury's "Illustrated Man."

Julian dressed, left for school and spent the entire day reminiscing about his dream. He almost pined for the night and the opportunity to have another—no—to experience *this* dream again.

When he retired for the night, Julian couldn't sleep. His yearning for the dream was so intense that it kept him awake. The next morning he decided to exert himself as much as he could during the entire day, hoping to fall exhausted onto his bed at night. Immediately after a sparse and hasty breakfast—much to the amazement of his mother—Julian ran out of the house. He ran the entire way to school, stopping only once to catch his breath when the stabbing pain in his sides forced tears to his eyes. During phys. ed. class he surprised the coach by completing the entire calisthenics program – even though he was last to finish. He ran in the schoolyard at recess, ran all the way home after school. He was tempted to stretch out and immerse himself in Stephen King's "Insomnia" after finishing his homework and before coming down to supper, but instead forced himself to race along all the streets in the neighborhood on his mountain bike.

After eating he retired to his room and wanted to read a bit, but he nodded off, the book falling from his hands. He was just barely able to undress and wash. He fell asleep as soon as his head hit the pillow...

... and ran across a wide, open field. The wind sang in his hair and he felt each single blade of grass under his bare feet. A scent rose to his nostrils, exciting him and causing his mouth to water: a wild scent, yet hauntingly familiar. He ceased struggling to identify it and simply gave in to the sheer pleasure of feeling his tireless muscles exalt as he ran. He seemed to run farther than he had during the previous dream... This was truly strange: Julian knew he was dreaming. He leapt effortlessly over obstacles, running uphill as easily and swiftly as on an even plain. His last impression before waking—this time prior to the screaming of the alarm clock—was that of his face coming closer to the ground upon which he ran.

Julian held to his daily regimen with an iron will. Soon he noticed that he could push his body much further before fatigue overtook him than had been the case just a few weeks ago. Muscle began to form where only flab had been earlier and the phys. ed. coach complimented him highly—with respect for the boy in his eyes. Julian found that his newly gained fitness even allowed him the energy to read his beloved horror novels before going to bed despite of the physical activity he demanded of himself.

He didn't dream every night, but frequently—and each time the dream seemed to continue where the last one had ended. One night he began to experience his exhilarating dream and felt the blades of grass tickling his chops as he ... chops!? Julian looked down on himself and recognized broad, gray-furred paws caressing the ground almost silently with each swift step. The scent he had not totally recognized in the previous nights was completely discernable to him now: a mixture of blood and torn flesh—human flesh. The significance of his sleeping visions struck him almost as dramatically as a divine enlightenment.

He had dreamt he was a werewolf.

Thereafter, just as his classmates were beginning to seek his company, Julian withdrew himself systematically. His dreams grew increasingly more important to him. Only in these nocturnal flights did he experience the true meaning of freedom. This ... wisdom of nature separated him from his fellows; of that he was certain.

Soon summer vacation began. Julian was able to pursue the strengthening of his body without disturbance from anyone. His vigor, muscle power and stamina increased daily, but he was not able to enjoy his new vitality without a grain of salt. The comfort he had always found in the novels he so loved evaded him now. His pubescent life had taken a turn toward the melancholy. He did his best to ban the unquenchable desire, but it was no use. Julian Brockmill had only one wish.

He wanted to be a werewolf.

Julian was by no means insane. He knew very well that werewolves existed only in novels, but the longing to become one of them left him no peace. It grew; fiercely, desperately, until every waking moment caused him such anguish that it was all he could do to keep from screaming. Only one course of action remained for Julian.

He decided to end his suffering.

Julian lay awake this night. That reminded him of the night—now seeming so long ago—during which he had waited for the repetition of his first fateful dream. *If only I had known then what I know now* ... What? What would have changed? Would he have acted differently, had he recognized his yearning to become a werewolf earlier? Hardly. If anything at all, he'd have begun his rigid training even sooner. Julian regretted only the knowledge that all hope had left him: *I think I could live with unfulfilled yearning. But I know I can't live without hope.*

Without leaving a farewell letter or any other indication of what he was about to do, Julian boarded a bus the next morning and rode to the end of the line—the Che-Che-Pin-Qua Forest preserve. Here he planned to still his impossible craving once and for all. The bottle of sleeping pills he had removed from the 'secret' drawer in his mother's shoe rack bounced against his thigh with each step as he walked deeper into the wood. After a while the trees gave way to a clearing and Julian found himself on the edge of a broad, hilly meadow. It wasn't exactly the same as the open field in his dream, but a strong impulse overcame him. *Why not? I'm going to die now, anyway.*

Julian undressed and folded his clothes into a neat bundle, placing them at the base of a fragrant pine. He turned in all directions, inhaling and exhaling the spicy air deeply several times before breaking into a run over the meadow. The flowing movements of his thoroughly trained body almost gave him pleasure. The wind in his hair *almost* transmitted the ecstatic feeling he had experienced in that first delicious dream. The grass beneath his feet and his easy speed seemed *almost* to cheer him on. As Julian leapt over a slight rise and increased his tempo, a barely perceptible rustling of joy tugged at his consciousness.

In spite of his decision to end his life, Julian almost laughed as he bent his knees slightly and vaulted—without touching the ground—over the ridge of the hill. Running down the other side, his speed increased. The blades of grass tickled his chops and ... *No. Can it possibly be true!?* Julian braked abruptly, stretching all four paws forward to come to a halt. Unbelievingly, he touched a powerful foreleg with his snout.

I've done it! For several minutes, Julian sat on his haunches halfway down the hill and tried to grasp the fact that he had apparently transformed himself into a werewolf through an act of sheer will. His intellect could not accept this, but he saw and *smelled* his body. His senses, grown so keen, left no room for contradiction. Only a wolf could hear and smell as intensively. Julian heard the ants crawling through the grass, smelled the mating of two moles beneath the earth in a hole next to his left forepaw. As he turned to take cover among the trees and try to determine what would happen next; whether he would have to transform back into a human from time to time, or... he caught the irresistible scent of prey.

Human prey.

His mouth watering, he felt the instincts of the wild animal take control. Peering downhill, he observed a small boy playing alone on the meadow. His parents must have been somewhere in the vicinity, but Julian could only pick up their scents weakly. They were too far away to disturb him. Carefully, slowly, silently he circled to move downwind of the child; but then it occurred to him that humans had dull noses indeed. Such precaution was exaggerated. The triumphant certainty of the successful predator rising within him, Julian simply ran down the hill toward the boy, leaping to attack when he came within range.

The child looked up in surprise, but it was too late. He scrambled awkwardly to his feet and began to scream for his parents as he ran a few, clumsy steps, but Julian was upon him and brought him down easily. The boy fell to the ground hard under Julian's compact weight and landed on his back. Julian jumped immediately onto his breast and buried his teeth in the boy's soft throat. The child gargled once, briefly and lay still. Julian lifted his bloody snout into the air and howled his victory toward the trees. In spite of the wonderful taste of hot blood on his tongue, Julian was surprised that his voice hadn't sounded like the voice of a wolf at all. He also observed that he possessed neither paws nor sharp claws, but rather human arms and hands covered with a light down and goose bumps instead of luxurious fur. Although his teeth were also those of a human—and had not for one moment been anything else—that was of no importance. The little boy lay dead on the ground, his throat torn open.

Learning to Swim
Marcia Biasiello

Whenever I run away, I never leave the house. I just go inside my bedroom closet and crouch down on the floor to fit in here. I pull the door closed from the inside and lie all the way down and bend my knees up. My feet touch the hems of my skirts and pant legs hanging from the rod up at the top of the closet. I push all of my shoes to the back wall and feel around in the dark for a sock to stuff under the door so that no one can pull it open from the other side. After a while my eyes adjust and then I take out my diary and the flash light I keep locked in a metal box in here. I wrote on the very first page as soon as I got my diary *You are FORBIDDEN from ever reading this!* It's where I write all of my feelings.

I used to be able to tell my mother all of my feelings, but not anymore. Not since she started working at the shelter for runaway teens. Every month she stays at her job one night to answer the teen hot-line. She likes to figure out what people should do with their lives. Maybe one of those teens will listen to her advice sometime. Then she'll feel like she's helped someone. But my mother doesn't realize what's important, at least not to me. *My mother says I'm too young to want a boyfriend. She said she won't watch her daughters ruin their futures by getting tangled up with boys before we even try doing something on our own. She said we should know what it's like to at least try. She says, "Don't just go giving your life away because some boy smiles at you." Maybe, in her opinion, working at Baker's Pharmacy and Cosmetics, where my sister works, is one way to keep your life from going in the wrong direction. But that's not the direction I see being a good one for myself. And maybe my sister doesn't really want that for herself, either. She just can't tell my mother that.*

Sometimes I hear my mother calling me when I'm in here, "Suzie..." I hear her heels on the wood stairs. And then they get quiet when she gets to the carpet in my bedroom. "Susan?" I hear her going from my room to my sister's bedroom and then to the bathroom, opening and closing the doors, trying to see where I am. "Susan Jane!" And then she goes back down the stairs again, one heel after the other.

The screen door slams shut and flaps a couple of times. Once she's outside, I let my breath out. When her voice trails off far enough away from the house, I open the window and climb down the trellis. The vines scrape my wrists. When I get to the grass, I brush off my bare knees and call back to her. "Mom...I'm over here, Mamma. I'm pulling weeds." I don't really have to hide from her. Just from my sister. I don't want my sister to find out where I keep my diary.

I can't take my sister anymore. She watches everything I do. My diary is 200 pages. I'm gonna fill mine up before she ever finishes hers. I'm also going to have a real boyfriend before she does, too. Her diary looks exactly the same as mine. There's a rose embossed on the velvet cover. I can trace my finger on the flower in the dark. She gave me her extra diary so that I wouldn't tell my mother about last week.

Last week my sister never came to get me after school. I thought I saw her car from the bus shelter where I get dropped off, but she never turned onto the road where I was waiting. I ran out to the highway to see of that was her car but it was gone by the time I got there. I thought I saw her turn onto the road across the river, but I couldn't tell if it was her for sure. I waited a little while longer, but she never came back. I decided I should walk home in the grass along the side of the highway if I was ever gonna get home that night. Most of the way, I walked backwards so I could see if one of the cars coming was hers. I would've waved my hands to stop her if I saw her drive past again, but I didn't recognize any of the cars that passed me. It started raining. And thundering. The road from the bus stop winds around three farms before it gets to our house. Our house is an extra one on the Johnson's farm that we rent from them. It could use some paint on the outside especially, but my mom said she's too tired to paint someone else's house after working at her own job. They don't ask us do any chores and they let us climb their trees and eat as many of the apples that we find on the ground as we want. When you walk home from the bus stop in the rain, water from the road splashes up onto your face and legs when the cars go by. The mud sucks the shoes off of your feet into the wet ground. It was especially bad that night because I was wearing my sister's shoes that I forgot to ask her if I could borrow. If someone did pull over and ask if I needed a ride, I would go into a farmer's field because I don't go for rides in strange cars.

I'm on page 37 in my diary. Any time I write in it, I have to fill at least three pages before I put the book away or else it's bad luck. *Thirteen is a complete waste of time. When you turn 14, you get to graduate from eighth grade. But even then you still have to wait two more years until you're 16 to get your driver's license. That's three years from now, so I have to stand around and wait for my sister to remember that it's her turn to pick me up.*

My sister told me that if I ever did tell my mother about that night, she would tell my mother she can prove that I have a crush on Dale Fortune. She said she had to work late that night. That it wasn't her fault her boss made her stock the make-up and it took longer than her shift. She said when she came to get me I was gone. And that there's lots of cars that look like hers.

Dale's house is on the river across the bridge from the bus shelter. I know he notices me. *I've never seen Dale's hands up close. But I can tell when I watch him from across the river when he's working on his car that his knuckles are soft. They would feel different than the rest of his hands if you touched them. He has very long fingers. Sometimes a little dirt gets under his nails, but not enough to make them look like they aren't clean. He lays on the driveway on his back in the sunlight blasting "I'm Not Your Stepping Stone." He rubs sand paper around and around in trance circles. The dust sparkles fall off of the metal onto his face. I'm gonna play him my favorite Monkee's song, "I'm a Believer." He has to keep running his fingers from his forehead through his blonde hair to keep it out of his eyes.*

He's not my boyfriend, not yet. *I'm not allowed to have crushes.* My sister says that since she was never allowed to hang around with boys by herself until she was in high school, that I shouldn't be allowed to, either. She says that I can try and hide the fact that I am in love with Dale from my mother, but I can't keep a secret from her. She told me she sees everything I do, day or night. I tell her that she should mind her own business. That it's boring that she spends so much time thinking about what I'm doing. She should try doing something for her own self instead of watching me. Last night when we were eating the supper our mom left out for us, I told my sister to spend more time worrying about her own problems. That if she did, she might have a happier life. And then, maybe somebody would like her. Maybe even me. But not now. Not the way she is.

This is my sister's day to drive me to the bus stop before she goes to work. My mother usually drops me off except for the nights when she's away. When I get to the bus stop before school, the moon is still in the sky. When it's cold, the shelter is the only place to get out of the wind. It pelts on the tin roof like a cyclone. When it's raining, I stand inside facing forward, looking out at the flooding street. Or I sit in the corner on one of the pieces of the wood that someone stuck in there to make a seat. When it's not raining, I go over to the bridge to see if Dale is outside in his yard. If he is, I watch him. *Dale's eyes are blue like Caribbean water. I've seen pictures of the ocean. Someday, we'll go to the beach* together. And swim. Dale Fortune is a good swimmer. I saw him fall off his water skis into the river. I've never gone in water deeper than my waist. My mother doesn't want me going near the river until I learn how to swim. She said we don't have money for swimming lessons yet, but when we do she'll take me to learn at the public pool. So, for now, she doesn't want me trying to learn on my own. But water feels soft. When you walk out past the shallow part and lay down and stretch your arms and your legs out together, you stay on top of the water like an upside-down frog. You forget that you usually walk around on land. My sister doesn't care about nature, just about make-up and things you unwrap from packages. The kids I ride home with live in the subdivision. When we get dropped off, they disappear into front doors, or pair off down gravel roads, and fade behind trees with no plans of ever going home.

Even though the alarm clock in my sister's room is the loudest sound in the house, she oversleeps if I don't go into her room and call her. I unplugged her clock last night. I'm not going to wake her up today. When I finish this page I'm gonna get my bike out of the garage and ride down to the bridge. Dale might be outside. My sister will lose her job at Baker's and it will be my fault. But then she'll have more time to look for a boyfriend. Maybe he'll like her so much that he asks her to marry him. And that will be because I helped her. The older you get, the harder it is to help your sister. I think she should find someone who pays attention to when she puts time into her hair style and notices that she's wearing perfume. Someone like Dale.

I can tell from the light under the closet door that it's later in the morning than when I go to school. The moon must have gone back into the sky. So why is my sister's voice in the yard? "Suuuuzie...get up. You're late for school." The screen door slams shut and flaps a couple of times. I hear feet on the stairs. I'm shoving my diary back into the box and open the closet door. I stood up so fast my eyes went hazy. "I don't have time to drive you today. Get your books. Mom left you a ham sandwich downstairs on the counter. Why aren't you dressed for school yet!" she yells and rushes out of my room. I pull my school sweater over my head and follow her into her room. She's taking her clothes off and throwing them against the wall. She's hopping around the room, pulling her uniform on one leg and then the other. Her bed looks exactly how it did last night when I said good night to her and she was sitting on the floor painting her toenails pink. I follow her down the stairs. There's a car in the driveway behind hers. It looks familiar but I'm rushing so much that I can't recognize it. She said someone else is going to drive me to school today. She opens the car door, "Just get in. I'll meet you at the bus after school tonight." She smells like perfume. "Dale Fortune is driving you to school today. And you can't tell Mom. I'll bring you some lipstick home from Baker's."

"You know Dale?" I ask her. Dale rolls down the window from the driver's seat and rests his elbow on the door. "Dale," I say, "are you really driving me to school?"

"Sure," he says, "unless you'd rather go swimming. I bet you like to swim."

"Kind of. Have you ever been to the Caribbean?"

My sister leans down to look at me through Dale's window. She's saying, "You'll be late for school but I called them and told them we had car trouble. You can't tell anybody, Suze."

"Okay," I say.

"Thanks for doing this," she says to Dale. And he reaches his long fingers around my sister's neck. "You can't tell anyone, Suzie" she says. Dale pulls her face against his and presses his mouth tight against hers. My sister is kissing Dale Fortune. My sister knows Dale. I told her about him. She never said anything about him being a boy she saw herself. Only someone that I love.

"I don't ride in strange cars," I say and open the car door.

"Susie, you have to get to school." my sister grabs me by my wrist, but I grab hers and pull it off of mine.

"Your car smells like mildew. And sickening perfume." I kick the door shut and run into the corn field. I'm not going to stop running. I'll keep running through the broken cornstalks until I get to the river. And then, I'll go past the shallow parts and lie down on my back and stretch out my legs and arms. But this time, I don't care, I'm going to turn over and do strokes and breathing. Today I am going to make it across the river.

⋮

30

⋮

The Kite
Evan Guilford-Blake

The kite rose and rose in the pale blue April air. It shuddered in the breeze and swooped, dusting the edges of clouds, chasing them like an eagle in pursuit of doves. Higher it went, a rippling mirror reflecting the shimmer of the day, higher, a silver window glistening in the sun, now higher still, a perfect diamond, all facets gleaming in the chamois-soft polish of the sky.

On the airless earth, Aubrey stood in the sand and watched the kite drift, his hands gripping the string as it slipped roughly through them. *Fly*, he thought to it; fly away, up and away, over the earth, the mountains, the forests and the seas. *Fly.*

The kite flew; like a cool silver-winged bird it glided, its sleek body erect, its tail taut and showing many hues. The string pulled up into the wind, the same wind that gently blew Aubrey's fine blond hair across his smooth face and scattered it in random shadows along his forehead. In the pull he felt the kite's ache as it drew farther from him and closer to the sun. I belong *here*, it whispered to him from its throne. Not down there, it swayed; I am of the sky, of the wind. I am free. *Here* is where I belong.

At times the pull was so hard Aubrey could barely hold the spindle. Once the kite dragged him forward toward the water, his arms were lifted and he had to tug furiously to bring them back, to bring back the spool, to hold the kite from its flight.

No, it cried on an upward gust of wind. Don't stop me; let me go, or come with me. Yes, and we will fly together, in the stars and through the clouds, we will soar, we will float on the music of the moon...

"Aubrey. It's time to go." His mother's voice.

No, no; come...

"Aubrey. Wind up the string. Come on; aren't you hungry?" She came toward him with a smile and a wave, her short hair, pale as his, fluttering in the breeze.

Small and angular, she stepped lightly across the sand. He looked at the kite a moment longer, squinted to see as it dipped and sighed into the horizon. Then he pulled and it came, slowly, unwillingly, into his arms.

His mother took his hand. "*I'm* starving," she said and stroked his head. "So is Dad. OK?" He nodded. They walked toward the car.

"You flew that thing really well," his father said as they drove home. "When *I* was seven I couldn't even get one in the air." Father's deep laugh filled the car with one of Aubrey's favorite sounds. "Of course, when *I* was seven I didn't have a fancy new silver kite that seems like it's born to fly. No, sir."

"It's pretty." Aubrey adjusted the kite beside him; at rest now, it seemed frail and hapless, the mylar dull and limp, the tail that Aubrey had made himself from an old tablecloth lying listless across the seat. "It talks to me."

"Oh, does it?" Father said. "What does it say?"

"Things." He sat forward and said urgently, "Things about flying, what it's like to be up there, with the clouds and stars and things." Then softly, "It says it wants to fly away." Mother laughed. "It does," Aubrey insisted.

"Yes, dear," she said gently. "There are always words on the wind."

That evening, when Aubrey was in bed, she sat on the back porch and watched his father lay bricks for the new patio. He hummed as he lifted them with powerful hands and arms, laying them with a delicacy that always surprised her, a delicacy that reminded her of her son. She laughed and he turned, grinning through his sweat. "What?"

"Oh, just what a wonderful imagination Aubrey has, John."

His father answered, "Yes. He certainly does."

The moon peered through the boy's open window. He lay awake and stared at the kite that leaned from its hook, silver on a silhouetted cross. It rustled, then quietly shivered, rocking side to side on its mount. He closed the window; at last, the kite lay still and Aubrey slept.

April warmed to May, the days grew longer, the sky deeper. He added another ball of string to his spindle and the kite dived into the deepest part, bobbing from time to time into Aubrey's sight, then teasing, disappeared again. He let the string out slowly and the kite agreed, enjoying the anticipation until finally it knew there was no more and then it pulled and strained, no longer, he felt, to break away but to let him know what it was like to be there, to tell him where it wanted to fly, to ask him to come along. He wanted to; and, he knew, it wanted him. Once, when his parents were in the lake, swimming and laughing, he called softly, *how?* The kite sang back, *Just climb. Hold me as I lift you.* A burst of air shocked him forward and up. He clutched the spindle as his feet left the ground for an instant, and then he was frightened and shouted "no" loud enough that his mother came rushing from the water to ask what was wrong.

"Nothing," he told her. "I just thought the string was going to break."

"I won't," the kite murmured to him from a thousand feet above, its tail waving reassurance. I won't leave *you.*

———

"What will you do this summer?" Miss Condon asked the class in June. "Go to camp," Andy Boburka answered; "Visit Gran'pa's farm in Indiana," Rhea Bradbury told her; "Swim and play baseball and help my dad make hamburgers on the grill," said Roxanna Lacy.

"What about you, Aubrey? Are you going away this summer?" Miss Condon asked.

"I don't think so," he said. "Probably just to the lake sometimes."

"Well," his teacher said, "then you'll go swimming and have picnics and skip stones," she said brightly. "That will be fun."

He nodded. "And I can fly my kite. Way, way up. All the way up to the sun."

Miss Condon smiled and raised her eyebrows. "That," she said, "is a long way up indeed."

———

The beach was crowded. Everywhere small children kicked up sand as they squealed across its grainy heat and into the water. They splashed cool droplets across sandy bodies, watched the drops run bead along their lotioned arms and chests. Everywhere adults stretched out on blankets, urging the sun onto their backs or keeping time to music while they laughed and pulled icy cans from styrofoam chests. Everywhere dogs chased frisbees, and teenagers tossed footballs or beachballs or danced, their bare feet skimming the sand as they moved.

Among them all, Aubrey stood, his gaze fixed upward, searching. It was Independence Day; that night there would be fireworks, and the sky, the kite's world, distant and sapphire and pearl as the one on which he stood was topaz and jade, would be flecked with spangles of gold, of copper, with showers of phosphorescent platinum and cinnabar and brass. And in the sparks would be a single one of silver, one which now skated in graceful figures-eight farther than Aubrey's eyes could see, but whose laughter slipped down the high wire between them to his hands, his ears, and caroled mysterious melodies in his mind. *Tonight*, it urged—will you be with me above the firelight, a part of the glow? We will rise with the moon and race beside a comet. Will you come, will you come?

Yes said Aubrey to the sunlight. I will come.

—┬—┬—

"Aubrey. Are you ready yet?" His father called from downstairs.

"Almost."

"We'll be in the car. C'mon. We don't want to miss anything."

"OK," He called back, and thought excitedly, I won't miss *anything. We* won't.

He put on his cap and looked at the kite. It hung motionless, the spindle beside it. He took a deep breath and blew as hard as he could; the kite rippled and crackled into life, dancing like a skeleton on its hook. He waited till it quieted again, then lifted it off gently, and held it to his face. The face that looked back at him was theirs: his own features, round and soft, pocked by transparent patches where the mylar had peeled, and ruddy spots where the wind and sun had parched the kite's complexion. One eye was missing, his mouth was a singe of brown above his chin. He smiled; the singe curled and wrinkled.

Aubrey ran across his room holding the kite by its bow; it snapped at the thin air, trying to rise on it. At his door he stopped and turned out the light. "I'm ready," he said softly. In his hand the kite was still. Carefully, he went downstairs.

—┬—┬—

"What are you going to do with that?" his father asked as Aubrey climbed into the car.

"Fly it. Fly with it." He fidgeted in the back seat.

"You're going to fly? During the fireworks?"

"Uh-huh. We're going to watch them from the sky," he said exuberantly.

"Oh," said his father. He laughed easily, and his mother joined. "Well, that'll be different. No wonder you can't sit still—sounds exciting."

"Yes," Aubrey answered. "It will be."

—┬—┬—

It was dusk when they got there, just beginning to blacken. The lake was already dark save for the headlights of approaching cars, the glint of an occasional match or the concentric dazzles of a whorling sparkler beneath the moonless, starless sky. They spread their blanket above the beach, in the shadows of the pines and cedars which surrounded it. The small bluff was almost empty; the crowd was below, a dozen deep on the beach; or on the lake itself, away from the pier where the rockets and Roman candles lay waiting for the night once it settled, confident and poised in its black domain.

There was only a slight breeze. Will it be enough, Aubrey wondered, softly aloud; beside him on the grass, the kite rustled. It would; he smiled, watching his dad light a sparkler that threw its glittered needles into the air, dotting the kite with pricks of shimmer.

The night settled; no more headlights and on the beach, there was the hush of anticipation. The moon peeked through a cloud a moment, cast a halo around the scene, then vanished again like a ghost. Aubrey lifted his kite. "I'm going to fly now," he murmured into the stillness.

"Don't go too far," his mother cautioned. "Stay on the bluff. Oh, look."

A Roman candle startled the darkness, erupting in a fountain of white, raining rillets of fire over the water, then sinking in gray smoke through the sky. Aubrey watched it fall, raised the kite behind him and raced away, feeling it tug, grasp the air, hold it, and then, at once, streak into the night, a silver skyrocket on ivory thread that spun through Aubrey's fingers like flax through a wheel. "Yes," he cried aloud. "Yes. Fly."

He stopped running and turned to watch its rise. Already the kite was a bare outline, high above him and rushing upward, a star taking flight. A hundred feet, two hundred, five, a thousand and still it climbed. From the beach there was an "ahh" as a catherine wheel exploded, scattering mercurial pinwheels across the night. Twelve hundred feet, *fifteen* hundred, eighteen. The string spun, and spun, and stopped.

And then he felt it. At first the pull was gentle, like being drawn from sleep on a summer morning. Without meaning to, he took a step, upward it seemed, and then another, and another, and suddenly his arms stretched in their sockets, he held the spindle with all his might and will, and another step and he rose and rose, up, up, his feet brushed the tops of trees and he climbed, up the string and through the sky and he heard the kite, its laughter, its music, and he sang with it, *free, away, away.*

Below him he saw the lake shining purple and green, then yellow and blue, then white. He swirled, the kite whirled him in circles and he danced with the wind. Higher, and the lake was a pond surrounded by moving dolls and lit by flashing colored bulbs, Christmas lights sparkling through miniature trees around the shore. Higher, and it was a pool, circled by a garden he saw only by match lights. He entered a cloud and a world of gray, then passed through it and saw the moon, the moon full and frosty in the company of stars.

———

Over the lake, the fireworks ended in a blaze of red and gold. Applause mingled with the smell of sulphur hanging thickly in the air. Then darkness, and then light again, sudden and brightly intrusive as headlights burst through the blackness. People packed blankets and ice chests into trunks and drove away, no longer looking at the sky but talking of it, of its breathtaking splendor and wonderful glow. On the bluff, his mother turned to his father and said "It was the best they've ever had. Don't you think so?"

"Spectacular. Even better than last year, huh, Aubrey?" He turned, but saw no one. "Aubrey," he called into the dimness.

"Oh, him and that kite." She sighed and shook her head. "John, he probably ran to the beach for a better view. I *told* him to stay on the bluff."

"Let's find him," his father said and stood up. He brushed the sand from his slacks, circling the bluff and the beach with his gaze. "Nowhere!" he muttered with a touch of exasperation. "Well, he can't have gone too far." He rolled their blanket and together, they walked down the bluff onto the warm beach, calling his name again, and again, to the earth.

Above them, in the sky, Aubrey heard only the wind and the darkening laugh of the kite. *Farther*, it commanded, and pulled. He felt his cap fly off, his hair stream back in a pennant; he clutched the spindle as the kite flew, flew, faster, higher and faster. *No*, he screamed, but the sound was lost in the kite's laughter as the earth below hurtled by too quickly to be seen and the sky became an ocean, impenetrable, endless, eternal. Deeper, deeper, they plunged.

Schemas
Tina V. Cabrera

Where do I begin? When did this madness begin to envelop me? Was it the antagonistic Denny's waitress, the aggressive bank teller or catching Billy jacking off on Playboy? Somewhere in the provisional instants of time we call memories, lies the epicenter of the tremulous ripples that sent me over the edge.

Astronomy 101. When I arrived late to class, I chose the metal chair in the back row, scooting it back to make room for my long legs. I rested my heavy backpack on my outstretched legs, forcing my battered heels against the floor. When Professor Astronomy flung the door open, sliding across the shiny, waxed floor that matched the bald spot on the top of his head, he was wearing the same tired t-shirt with the glow-in-the-dark planets and stars. I hated that shirt and the manner he took in his lectures, holding his skinny frame erect like a drill sergeant, seeing right through us as if we were transparent. He paused to place his briefcase on the table, tied the sparse strands of the tail of his ridiculous gray mullet into a ponytail, and pressed the button to lower the film screen.

The lights dimmed and the chapter on lunar eclipses appeared. I reached down for my study guide, and when I looked up, this is what I saw in glittering PowerPoint letters, appearing sequentially on the screen:

Y-O-U L-I-G-H-T U-P M-Y L-I-F-E

"It's karaoke time and we'll begin with my favorite, an oldie for you guys, not for me." He started belting out lyrics about having the hope to carry on in a crackly, falsetto voice. I looked around at my classmates; they began blurring in the foreground. I could not see their expressions, only of Fellow Student whose head was tilted back, his mouth hanging wide open. "It breaks the routine, yeah?" I turned away and felt my own face contort into disbelieving expressions.

Professor Astronomy raced up the steps, the nostrils of his long pointed nose flaring like a dragon, and lunged at Fellow Student, knocking him to the ground. "Drop and give me 50," he ordered. "And you, Young College Student, put this on," he said to me as he pulled off his tired shirt and handed it to me. The ripples of his ribcage were showing and I shut my eyes, but obeyed. Fellow Student counted, "Uno, dos, tres..." as he clapped his hands in between.

I ran towards the back door exit, not daring to look back. I nearly turned back, hoping to see Professor teaching as usual, pointing to the phases of the moon with his laser pointer—no matter how boring—pausing for questions. It was the questions that led to thoughtful speculations, and to more questions, which led to answers that at least made sense. But this—none of this belonged to any familiar framework in my head.

But this isn't where it began. Somewhere in these past two weeks, something must have been the trigger. By this time in class, my pasty skin needed washing, white flakes drifted from my itchy scalp, and I was wearing the same white shirt sullied from over-wear. I restlessly rubbed at the stubble growing on my chin and liked the scratchy feel on my fingertips, but not the hot row of acne bumps rising up my left cheek. I felt dirty. I hadn't slept much, and my life had already taken a turn into uncertainty, I'm certain.

Maybe it was Sunday breakfast at Denny's, the weekend before Astronomy 101.

Everything had begun as usual—the hostess leading me to a comfortable booth by the window, handing me the breakfast menu: "Your waitress will be with you shortly." I tossed the menu aside and ordered my usual—the Grand Slam. A new waitress walked towards my table, sliding into the booth right next to me, setting the iced water down. I looked at her lapel, which read, "Slam me!"

"How's it goin'?" she asked.

"Fine I guess," I answered, moving closer to the wall. "You're new here?" I said, clearing my throat.

"Slammy, slamoo, slam you!" she jingled. "Your hair looks like it's on fire!" She must have noticed the red I had Billy add to the tips of my blazing black hair. "And what are your plans for the weekend?" she asked as she got closer to me, planting me against the wall. I sat in uncomfortable silence, staring down at her apron pocket, hoping she would get up and take my order. Instead, her eyes rolled around, back and forth. "Goshitsbeen-aroughweekforme-I'vebeenonmyfeet-twentyfourseven-andimtiredofallthegriping." After each syncopated phrase, she sucked in air. I whirled around, looking for help. She stood up and lit a cigarette.

"Hey," I whispered, "there's no smoking inside." She swept the cigarette from her lips with two fingers and ground it into my right hand. I yelped in anguish, splashing the cold water onto my hand. Then I splashed the rest in her face as I pushed her aside and made for the exit. Her voice trailed off as she announced, "The pie of the week is..."

I suppose I could've run back in and complained to the manager, but I didn't. Act now, ask questions later. That's my way. So this must've been it. This was the first of the many strange events of the last two weeks, which pulled the rug from under me, and swept me into a world unknown and unfamiliar.

When I left Denny's all I could think of was how I needed more cash. So I drove to the ATM and punched my pin number in: 4, 2, 1, 6. That didn't work. So I tried, 4, 1, 2, 6. That wasn't it either. Was it 4, 6, 2, 1? I was blocked out of the machine. It spit out my card, so I went inside the bank.

"Next member please."

"Well, this is embarrassing, but I forgot my pin number and can't get any cash from the ATM. Can I withdraw $40, please?"

"Certainly sir," the male teller answered. I didn't like being called sir, but I found his tousled brown curls attractive, and his Adam's apple rippling up and down as he spoke. "It happens more than you would think, sir. Just fill out this form." It was odd that he was calling me sir, as I was still a young college student.

"Yeah, it's pretty funny actually," I said un-sir-like. "This has never happened before."

"Sir, just sign here please," he continued, annoying me despite the flash of his amazing blue eyes. "If you still can't remember your code later, just go to the customer relations desk and they will assist you in obtaining a new one." His manner was cordial, but uptight.

"Thanks, but I'm sure it will come back to me."

Yank. He pulled me by the collar and stuck his tongue in my mouth. I nearly choked, but the swirling of his tongue enthralled me, and he began sucking on my bottom lip. My heart beat rapidly as I both pulled away and drew in to him. He tightened his grip and I succumbed. But then just as easily he let go, and I collapsed to the floor. I edged backwards like a crab, sweating, and watched the teller as he carried on: "Next member, please."

Managing to hobble back onto my feet, I couldn't look up, out of shame. I felt for my lower lip but could only feel my fingertips. Trickles of sweat were blinding me as I struggled to the door. In the chaos of my mind, I could not remember where I had parked.

But despite the madness of these events, it was Billy. Billy sent me over the edge. Catching Billy just this afternoon in his bedroom, with the Summer Special Issue of *Playboy* in his hands. In one hand he held the magazine, and with the other, he was jacking off through the slit of his red-checkered shorts. I had gone into the kitchen a few minutes before to heat up rolled tacos in the microwave, and when I shoved the door open with my foot, I saw him yanking, pulling, his face squeezed like a pale prune. I shut the door without a word, laid the plate of tacos on the coffee table, and walked out of the place.

As I sat down in my car, sighing heavily, struggling to catch my breath, I felt a tingling sensation down my legs before they went numb. I felt the urge to climb back into the warmth of Mother's womb, to call out to her for help. But she didn't know about Billy and me. At least I didn't think so. And even if she did, what would she say? Would she be accepting? Instead of comforting me, she'd accuse me of abandoning her just like Dad did years ago. Ever since then, I've been her sense of security, the man of the house...

Maybe she'd suspected, that night a year ago when Billy and I first started seeing each other. That night we took a drive around downtown to spend some time alone. I kept my cell phone on silent, not even vibrate so I wouldn't feel it like a stun gun in my pocket through the night. Mom would always have some excuse to call, to remind me that we hadn't watched the rented videos yet that were due the next day, or that her home-cooked meal was waiting for me, getting cold. I didn't have a curfew anymore, but she always found some way to make me feel guilty that she was home alone again.

Billy drove that night, and dropped me off one or two houses away from mine, at my urging—just in case Mom was peeking through the blinds again. "Why do you worry so much?" he asked me, "She knows we're friends. You have friends." Maybe I was being paranoid, but I didn't want to make her suspicious. Billy and I had started off as friends. But then his common, small brown eyes grew uncommon to me. Deep and reassuring, they had a way of smiling at my eternally alarmed wide ones. Maybe Mom would catch on to this, a look passing between us. She's clairvoyant, Mom, with the uncanny ability to decipher the simplest expressions.

I had wanted to spend the night with Billy at his place that night, but knew that at eighteen years old, a sleepover would seem strange. And as I'd walked up my driveway, there was Mom, peeking through a small slit through the curtains. "That's odd," she said when I unlocked the door. "It's as if you just suddenly appeared. And your hair is all ruffled." I glanced at the round mirror hanging behind the door, and my normally perfect side part had indeed disappeared under disheveled tufts. "You didn't walk home, did you?"

"No Mom, of course not," I answered. I couldn't lie to her; I told her I had hung out with Billy.

"Hmmmm," she said, with a meditative look.

I'd looked away, making sure she couldn't study my face.

When I left Billy to his Playboy, I was tempted to go back inside, to give him a chance to explain. But my desire for Mom's warmth took over, and so I drove home.

After passing through the swinging wooden gate in the dark, I tried unlocking the door, but it was already unlocked. Strange, I thought. The fluorescent light didn't activate as usual, meaning Mom had not switched it on. She wasn't in the kitchen, and no food was on the table, covered and kept warm, waiting for me. The dishes were piled up in the sink. I tiptoed to check for a light coming through the slit under her bedroom door. None. Mumbling from the living room and the flicker of lights called to me in the darkness. She was sprawled on the couch, dozing in front of the hazy TV. "Mom, it's me. What's for dinner?" I asked.

She flinched, opened her eyes, gave me a quick once-over, and turned her attention back onto the T.V. screen. "That's not your shirt, is it." It was a statement, not a question.

"No Mom, it's not."

"Is it Billy's?" My heart beat rapidly again just as it had in the bank. Only it was out of fear rather than desire. Her voice was both sleepy and icy. I refused to answer that foreign tone coming from a familiar form and made my way to the couch, squeezing myself into the corner against the armrest.

"You're a fag, aren't you? You and Billy." Her freshly black-dyed hair was pulled back in a tight ponytail, rather than falling loosely onto her shoulders as it usually did. It made her slanted eyes look even more narrow. She was wearing her white terry robe, the one I remembered from childhood, still soft and white like lamb's wool. She looked as if she had shrunk, but she wasn't old enough to shrink like old people do. I wanted to shrink, lie safely on her shoulder back like I used to when I was small, while she watched her favorite shows from the corner of her eye. She hadn't really been watching, those lazy afternoons, but lulled into sleep by the constant streaming sounds.

And I was lulled too, by the rise and fall of her breathing. I rode safely into those sweet dreams of flying in a rainbow sky, or floating in the air. I could never remember waking up.

"God made Adam and Eve, not Adam and Steve," she continued, her voice rising in anger. "If everyone were gay, that would mean the end of the human race. Then what about natural selection, survival of the fittest? There would be nothing fit to survive. There's a frozen Hungry Jack in the freezer."

As I sit here, I don't know how many hours have passed. Mom still lies there in the same position, her eyes now shut. The TV's no longer hazy, and scenes from the ten-o'clock news are flashing, one after the other. The shadows and colors on the screen palpitate and pulse, mimicking the electrical pulses of my unstable heart.

Mother, you are the center of my madness. But the chill in the room is beginning to settle into my skin, melting into recognizable warmth. The right words will surely form on my tongue, and finally release. Everything that has taken me by surprise will, like all things, become used and familiar. A frozen Hungry Jack doesn't sound so bad after all.

The Jameson's Bash

Amanda Caverzasi

Rani Singh, grand niece of the late hotelier magnate, Naresh Singh, had "achieved" middle age, or so she told her daughter, her heart-mate, Shoori, over the phone. Shoori, a college student in upstate New York, impatiently stirred her coffee, her spoon sounding against the ceramic mug. Her mom could be annoying. For instance, she had told friends and family in Bangalore that Shoori attended school in Manhattan and dated a six-foot-something blue-eyed blonde named Ryan. Last phone call, Shoori had finally set her mother straight, especially on the matter of Ryan, Shoori's Resident Advisor. Irate and guilt-ridden in turn, Shoori and her mother had ended up slumped on the floor, in tears. Since then, they had only dared discuss the lightest matters, in tender tones.

"Mom," Shoori sighed. "I've got to study for my exam on Friday."

"Daughter," Rani admonished. "I'm telling you an important story; one that I pray someday spares you pain."

Realizing she only prolonged her mother's call, Shoori quieted. Then, because her mother didn't speak, she said, "I'm here," trying to disguise the edge in her voice. "Go on," she said, more saccharine still. She considered substituting something stronger for her coffee but decided she'd treat herself later. For finishing the call. For bearing her mother. For doing her duty.

From her home facing M.G. Road, Rani began her story. Four days ago, at the Jameson's annual party, Rani Singh, age forty-nine plus, had realized her life's purpose.

Rani, and her husband, Pranit, Vice President of Sales for Singh Hotels, had met the Jameson's 18 years earlier in Singapore. They had relocated to that pristine, organized paradise for Pranit's career. Rani had immediately been incorporated into the expat community, a subset of the population that influenced Singapore's national identity. Led by Mrs. Jameson, Rani and the other expat mommies organized outings including Ballet Under the Stars at Fort Canning Park and shopping on Orchard road. For lunch, they usually met at the Raffles Grill. There they'd order rosé spritzers though, as Rani told Mrs. Jameson, she didn't think alcohol suited the Indian temperament.

In her fourth year in Singapore, around the time Shoori returned home from the zoo asking to adopt a bat the size of a Labrador puppy, Rani received a call from her cousin. Grand Uncle's health had declined. He could use Pranit in Bangalore. Preoccupied by her father's deterioration, the cousin, four years Rani's junior, said she felt old before her time. Rani, age 31 then, empathized. Since Pranit had turned 50, she had felt practically ancient. Though not usually so candid, Rani opened up to her cousin. After all, she thought her cousin had called for sympathy, not to tell her that Uncle Singh strongly recommended she come home.

The Singh's returned to Bangalore. Pranit's promotion and the cost of living in India meant they had a fortune. Still Rani found herself significantly less leisured. Caring for Pranit's aging mother and her increasingly independent-minded daughter demanded almost all of her time. Years passed, and Shoori left for college. By then, Rani had resigned herself to her role, household care-taker. Most of the time, Rani cheerfully performed her duties. Only once had she considered rebelling. On that day, she had actually felt her hair graying, fading as quickly as light streams through a fiber. Though that made Rani feel like snarling at Pranit and fleeing, she grounded herself, thinking this simple thought: Someday, if needed, she'd tell Shoori that everyone considers giving it up at one time or another. She'd say that faith in God helped one through the tough times.

Because Rani trusted that God looked after her, she hadn't been surprised to hear from Isobel Jameson so many years after leaving Singapore. Over the phone, Isobel told Rani that she had moved to the neighborhood. "You're not in India?" Rani had asked. "No, not quite. I'm in Bangalore." Isobel had replied, explaining that all the suits and Saudis made it impossible to consider Bangalore part of India. Isobel soon infiltrated Bangalore's expat community. Instead of organizing outings as she did in Singapore, she hosted brunches, game nights and her annual bash, a party held mid-March each year.

This year, Rani intended to go all out for Isobel's party. She persuaded Grand Auntie Singh to lend her a diamond pendant that had once belonged to Indian royalty. Then, on a trip to America, Rani purchased a party dress, an empire cut, aubergine Yves Saint Laurent that had been discounted several times. In the changing room, Rani had turned to check out her backside and the sheer outermost layer of her skirt had gently ballooned. Removing her glasses, she approached the mirror, chin leading so as to stretch the skin at her neck. Sure she had filled out over the years, but not as much as some of her friends. And though her upper arms could trouble her, Yves's capped sleeves covered them. Upon seeing her mother outfitted in the designer frock, Shoori had said, "Smoking hot, Mom."

In an effort to live up to Shoori's estimation, Rani had restricted her diet to ginger lemon tea and fruit, melon and dates mostly. Since last Monday, she had only snuck one small slice of Jarlsberg and a handful of baby carrots. On the day of the Jameson's party, she promised herself she'd fast, but by lunch on Saturday, she felt faint and so she stepped out to the local fruit stall for pears. Fruit in hand, Rani suddenly panicked. Considering that she planned to drape herself in Graff diamonds, she couldn't go to the Jameson's in her dress, an Off Saks purchase. She'd look as gauche as a little girl playing dress up.

— ⊥ — ⊤ —

"Shoori," Rani cooed. "Do you remember putting on your father's hat and sneaking around the house? Playing reconnaissance or something?"

Shoori grunted. Had her mother meant to insinuate that she had been a gauche eight-year old? Though offended, Shoori accepted the hit, hoping her silence might discourage her mother from starting on another tangent. Crossing the room, she tugged up her lounge pants. Then she tied a pony tail at the nape of her neck, so that it fell along her spine. She eyed the liquor she kept on the bottom shelf of her bookcase. Last Friday, her roommate had stocked up on Bailey's and other syrupy liquors, the stuff Shoori didn't care for.

"You can still be sneaky," Rani said. "Sly, I mean."

"So you returned Auntie Singh's pendant?" Shoori asked flatly.

"Cheeky girl," Rani replied, thinking she had raised her daughter right. "Clearly I couldn't go to Isobel's in that drape. You really ought to have stopped me from purchasing that shapeless monstrosity, My Dear. But I forgive you. So I stood outside that fruit stall thinking that I had nothing to wear to Isobel's and feeling faint. For fortification, I bit into the pear. I dribbled. A drop hit my forearm and ran. Since I didn't have a napkin or anything, I cleaned it best I could. Licking that stream of juice, I thought of substituting a razor for the tip of my tongue."

"Mom," Shoori exclaimed. "You're gruesome."

"It's only an allusion, Ma Puce."

"I mean you didn't bother peeling the pear before eating it?" Examining a bottle of Vox Raspberry, Shoori discovered that her roommate had already finished it.

"The skin is most nutritious, Jaan," Rani replied before returning to her story.

——

The rush of sugar to her brain had restored Rani. Tossing the pear core, she hurried to the nearest silk shop. Inside, Rani studied the cupboards of silks. Though the silks had been organized by color, Rani still found that looking through them dazzled her. Dabbing her forehead, Rani told a clerk that she needed a sari for the Jameson event that evening. Getting busy, the clerk pulled out a plum silk. Rani looked at him. "That shade doesn't suit me, Sir."

"Nonsense, Madam," said the clerk holding the material up to her face. "You're a picture."

"That's cute of you," Rani said, taking the material from the clerk and studying her reflection. "You think so?"

"Yes, Madam." The clerk blushed.

"I'm Rani." She dumped the silk into the clerk's hand. "You're?"

"Kunshi." Though he held the silk in the crook of his arms, he still managed to clutch Rani's hand.

"Let's try fuchsia, Kunshi."

But fuchsia didn't suit Rani. "It's better for my daughter," she told the clerk. "Of course she prefers muted tones."

The clerk tsked in sympathy, and Rani felt a surge of gratitude. Not everyone understood her as clearly as Kunshi did. She thought of Shoori's drab pony tail. So many times Rani had asked her daughter to fashion her hair high. "Like an Arabian horse," she had explained. Of course, Shoori never listened.

"Consider canary," Kunshi said, snapping open the silk material so that it spread across the counter. Rani ran her hands along the fine material and noticed a faint print, tiny golden crosses, or maybe stars, dotting the cloth. Recalling her studies in art history, Rani stepped back from the material as if studying a painting. Distanced, she could clearly see that the cluster of stars formed constellations.

"Would you?" Rani asked, holding up the material.

"Certainly." In seconds, the clerk had fashioned the cloth into a full length skirt that fanned out at his feet, forming a concentric circle. He pulled the silk tail diagonally across his chest and over his shoulder. Crossing the left knee over his right and thrusting his hip out, the clerk struck a feminine pose. Rani studied him critically. "Kunshi, my friend," she said. "Sold."

———•———

Considering she had selected her party outfit a mere four hours ago, Rani felt remarkably put together as she ascended the Jameson's marble staircase. Her hairstylist had created a soft chignon at the nape of her neck, and Rani had rimmed her eyes in kohl and colored her lips. Though she felt high, she put on a demure expression as she approached Mr. and Mrs. Jameson standing at the top of the stairs. "Rani," Isobel called out, grabbing Rani by her forearms and spinning her around so that Rani faced the guests ascending the stairs. "Splendid," Isobel said, looking at Rani's diamond pendant. "May I?" Rani nodded. Isobel lifted the pendant from Rani's chest, and then something strange happened. Minus the heft of the gem, Rani felt her heart fluttering fiercely. It pounded harder than it had earlier that afternoon, before meeting Kunshi. Rani took the gem from Isobel and returned it to her chest, holding it there. Invitation in her right hand, she fanned herself, feeling faint yet still present enough to pray that her perspiration hadn't stained her sari.

"Pranit," sang Isobel, seeing him saunter to Rani's side.

"Beautiful evening," said Pranit. He patted Rani's rump. Rani smelled the Jack Daniels on his breath, and it made her nauseous.

While exchanging pleasantries with Isobel, Pranit explored Rani over her sari. Slipping his hand into her crack, he grabbed her meaty buttocks. Though he reached her anus through layers of silk, Rani barely blinked an eye. Never a tall man, Pranit had shrunk over the years. Their daughter had to be nearly his same height, only a couple of inches taller than she was herself, Rani thought.

As if reading her mind, Isobel said, "Too bad Shoori's not here tonight. I suppose she takes after you, Pranit—she's an explorer, longing to see other worlds. As for her reserve—I know she doesn't get that from Rani."

Pranit removed his hand from her rump, and Rani glanced at her husband's face. Though he regularly quenched himself, she could see flaking patches of dried skin.

"She's thinking of majoring in economics, I understand," continued Isobel.

"Yes," said Pranit. "Then she'll do her MBA."

Isobel turned to Rani. "I expected to see you wearing plum, you fox." She stepped back to take in all of Rani. "Indeed, I'd say you're smoking, Rani." Having plastered a smile on her face seconds ago, Rani tilted her head to freshen her expression. Isobel kissed Rani's frozen upturned cheek before excusing herself. "Enjoy the evening," said Isobel, starting to retreat but then returning. "The queue is shorter at the bar on the balcony." She touched Rani's forearm.

Though Rani's heart had quieted as soon as she had placed the diamond on her chest, she remained troubled by something she could not name.

"I need a drink," her husband muttered. "Where's that bar?"

Right then Rani caught sight of another canary-clad guest. Rani studied the plump matronly figure for a second before grasping that she had actually caught herself in Isobel's gilded-edged mirror. Though she caught her blunder almost immediately, she had already judged the lady in the mirror. Old and flabby, she could no longer stand erect under the burden of supporting her husband to the bar. Though she hadn't yet had a drink, Rani started giggling, louder and louder. In her mania, she sounded a high-pitched machine gun titter that Isobel later described as a hyena's snarl.

⁘

⁘

As Rani neared the end of her story, she feared her daughter might not understand and so she did what she did best; she made it easy for Shoori.

"You're not amused?" Rani asked, finishing her story. "You're far too young to be so serious, Shoori. Shoori?"

Since the sugary liquor had lodged the cap, Shoori tried opening the bottle of Bailey's using her teeth. Thus occupied, she did not immediately respond. In the lull, Rani thought, not for the first time, that 8,000 miles could distance a mother and daughter.

Denial
Jan Chronister

Moonlight slips
through heavy bedroom curtains.
Basket of sun dried laundry
emits an alien freshness.

Slurred by wine
my mind travels slow,
restless hands avoid
breasts,
twin moons,
maps charted
once a year,
revealing seas
and rifts
I'd rather just ignore.

Radium Girl
Jan Chronister

Painting clock faces
with radium,
sharpening the brush tip
between her lips,
she gets the idea
to paint her teeth
so lovers can see her smile
glowing in the dark.

She died a long time ago,
right after the second war,
her mouth a miniature Hiroshima.

⋮

50

⋮

Twin Dolls
Melinda J. Combs

Inches from the fireplace, Bridal Barbie lays face up, hair askew, her white veil warming from the heat. Simultaneously, Savannah and Jack rumble around the living room floor, scraping the tops of their heads against the coffee table legs, muttering *bitch* and *asshole* to each other. A couple of minutes later, their mother meanders out of the kitchen to stop her two littlest angels from killing each other.

And because the mother remembers that the latest issue of *New Age Parent* suggests dropping down to a child's level proves to be the "most meaningful and effective form of connecting," she squats in front of Savannah and Jack, meeting their almost identical blue eyes, and says, "This behavior will not be rewarded."

"But, Mom, he took my Barbie." Savannah's red hair glimmers with bits of beige carpeting.

Jack throws his arm around his mother's neck and says, "Yeah, Savannah. This behavior will not be rewarded. Mom said" and while he leans into her, she glances over him and into the kitchen, where her *Parental Guidebook* props open to Chapter 14: "How to Handle Twin Rivalry without Conflict, Ages Ten through Twelve" with specific passages highlighted in yellow for Jack and orange for Savannah.

"Mom said. Mom said. Is that all you ever say?" Savannah bounces her head left and right, rhythmic to each syllable.

"Savannah, don't imitate Jack. We don't like that behavior. Nor do I like you two playing with Barbie. She's not a role model. I would hope that your father would remember that I don't want *my* children, I mean our children, to buy into this false representation of a female that just perpetuates our gender's oppression. He knows I don't approve, especially this bridal version. I'm shocked he bought her. Barbie's out with the recycling."

"But what about the new Ken? Is he a role model?" says Jack.

"No. He's also inappropriate."

"But Dad said Ken's been away to soul search."

"Is that what your father calls it these days?" She clears her throat.

"Mom, are you angry? Do you need to talk?" asks Savannah.

"No. No. I do not. No. Thank you very much." She clears her throat again.

Before her mom could finish, Savannah swipes the doll off the mantle and says, "Bridal Barbie's mine. All mine. "

Barbie's dress falls over her head, revealing her skin-colored, embossed, attached panties. Jack stares.

"Stop, you two. Please appropriately apologize to each other."

"I am sorry for my behavior, Jack."

"I am sorry for *my* behavior, Savannah."

And with that, the mother gives the twins air kisses and whooshes them outside, ordering them to make snow angels, and scampers back into the kitchen to finish decorating cookies for her eldest daughter's high school peace rally.

"Don't forget your coats before going outside," she says from the kitchen.

Just as the front door closes behind them, Jack growls, "You bitch." He heard that word on TV, probably Fox. His father lets him watch.

A minute later, Savannah runs down the driveway, coming to a stop on the sidewalk to face her brother. As she waves Bridal Barbie out in front of him, her hair, under the veil, whooshes from side to side. Her white floral barrettes fly away in every direction. Barbie's blonde hair holds Savannah hostage.

"Gimme that!" Jack reaches out for the doll.

"She's mine, and you know it!"

"Give me Barbie back. Now. I like her more than you do, Savannah." With a quick heave, Jack pushes Savannah backward. She lands on her rear end, her lower half getting damp from the snow. Rolling to her belly to cover Barbie with her body, Savannah lay motionless, waiting for her brother to stop. Jack kicks his sister in the ribs—his wet tennis shoe makes a footprint on her pink overalls. She rasps a breath out onto the snowy concrete.

"Hey, whatcha two munchkins doing?" Mr. Potter, the next door neighbor, asks.

"We're playing a new game. It's called Tackle for Barbie. We made it up this morning. I'm winning," Jack says with his hand patting his chest and his foot anchoring Savannah's ribs to the ground.

Mr. Potter continues to shovel the snow from his driveway, but nods his head and says, "Isn't that swell? I'm playing a game today with Mrs. O'Leary. Have fun, kids." And he takes his plaid wool cap off, waving it around for Jack, as if he has won the Kentucky Derby.

"Get off of me. Please." That word, the magic word, signals a truce. "Please. I need to be heard," Savannah asks. Her voice trails off at *be heard* since she remains belly down on the driveway.

"Fine. Be that way." Jack slowly releases his foot.

Snow starts to fall again.

Savannah, now clutching Barbie by the head, pushes herself up from the sidewalk, turns to face Jack and kicks him in the balls. He tumbles to the ground, falling down with a thud and moan.

"What the hell did you do now, Savannah?" says Sienna Joy. The older sister, en route to the bus stop, walks out the front door, noticing Jack on the ground while Savannah sticks her tongue out at him.

"Hey, you, you little demon, what did you do to your brother?"

"He fell over." Savannah bends over to pat Jack's back.

"Jack, is that true?"

"She went past my personal zone. I need to talk about my feelings."

"Cut the shit. Just answer the question." Sienna Joy lights a cigarette, holding the match out to see if it would go out from the snowflakes. She always smokes before her Sunday afternoon shift at the diner.

As Jack rolls over, cupping his groin with his hands, he says, "The bitch kicked me in the balls."

"He's lying again."

"You two suck shit. I've had it." And with a flourish of her cigarette, Sienna Joy stomps past them, crunching the snow with her boots. She doesn't go back in the house to talk to their mother about the twin's latest antics or offer to help bake the peace rally cookies.

"You bastard." Jack slowly stands up, pulling his pant seam out from between his legs. He spies Bridal Barbie, her sequined bodice peeking out of Savannah's front overall pocket. She has secretly placed Barbie in there while on her belly—Jack never saw her move.

"Die, brother!" And with that proclamation, Savannah leaps up and kicks her brother in the face—she learned that move from Power Rangers, a show their mother forbids them to watch due to its "excessive and inappropriate fighting." Savannah practices the move every night before bedtime.

Jack's head flies back and his left front tooth chips in half. He swallows the other half. His head rolls forward and his eyes sear, staring at his sister. In one quick motion, he kicks one foot forward enough to buckle Savannah's knees. She hurls forward, trying to land on her brother to take him down with her, but he dodges her by mere seconds.

This time while on the ground, before she can roll over to protect herself, Savannah feels a huge crush of weight on her side—Jack practices a Gutwrench Powerbomb, a move learned from watching Smackdown while on weekends with his father. He springs back onto his feet immediately after crushing his sister's side. With three broken ribs, Savannah starts to cry, but just as she does, Jack reaches in her pocket to grab Bridal Barbie, but his hand, so close to her face, is clenched by her teeth. She wraps her mouth around his wrist, closing her jaw. Jack kicks Savannah again, but this time, she grabs his heel and yanks upward, forcing Jack to the ground. His wrist is freed from her grip. Teeth marks pock his skin.

"Savannah, I hate you," Jack says, while punching her in the stomach.

"No, I hate you more," spitting blood on Jack's shoes. Her entire front tooth has disappeared. She reaches her hands around his neck. He does the same. They both land in a heap on the driveway, rolling around from one side of the driveway to the other, and within a few moments, Bridal Barbie falls out of Savannah's pocket and rolls down the driveway into the gutter.

A few minutes later, the twins lay motionless.

Mud soaks Bridal Barbie's hair and stains spot her virginal dress. Her white shoes are buried somewhere under the snow, never to be found again.

When Mr. Potter and Mrs. O'Leary walk his dog, Ace, they hasten past the Parker's home; it's time for *Wheel of Fortune*, so they don't notice the only twins on the block sprawled out on their driveway, partially covered in snow. But Ace catches a whiff of the doll, snatches her up, carrying her by the leg all the way home. That night, he buries Bridal Barbie in the backyard.

The Day I Brought the Wild Boy Home
Darla Crist

The Day I Brought the Wild Boy Home you said that I could keep him. I've got the conversation right here, on my Panasonic tape recorder, the one you gave me for Christmas. You said I could keep him, and I did, all summer, as my field journal will attest:

Day 1. The wild boy falls from our walnut tree, without even a gasp or a whimper. On each of his shoulders is a curved white scar in the shape of a magnet or fish hook. He appears to be a nocturnal creature.

Day 2. In the morning, the wild boy naps in the closet, nested in boxes of silverfish bait. His teeth are white against the brown of his face. It hurts to look there. The wild boy. Shining.

Day 3. He insists on drinking milk from a saucer.

Day 8. He smells of melted wax and the grit of cedar ashes.

Day 10. My thoughts drift up to the rafters like smoke.

Day 19. We test the rhombus of the swimming pool. He unfolds in the water and defines efflorescence.

Day 21. You make a comment at breakfast about the milk saucer on my floor.

Day 28. I am drawn to the green-tinged rim of the pond, where the leaves are trying to float out a sentence. The wild boy arranges the leaves with a stick. What is it the wild boy is trying to say?

Day 32. We stand beneath a Chinese lantern, dispersing the kisses of gnats and moths. The wild boy and I, pearled orange and pink. He leans against me. Smiling.

Day 36. The wild boy sleeps with his mouth flung open. There is no sign of silver fillings. The postman causes the wild boy to cringe. Apparitions continue to bring the mail.

Day 41. The wild boy exhibits a fear of beehives. He seems to think daylight is kept inside; Song of the bee clan, endlessly turning. One golden creature. Shining.

Day 42. I consult a map of the United States, spread out like a prayer on the mercy of the table. I search for migratory patterns of wild boys and geese. He does not divulge his name or his kin.

Day 51. My spine starts to hum like an uncharted forest. Words return to me as particles of glass.

Day 52. The wild boy is the key to moonlit houses. What is it the wild boy is trying to say?

Day 57. The wild boy cannot be photographed. I am left with a curtain and a Boston fern.

Day 65. We take to the trees and are scolded by neighbors. I learn that falling is what civilizations do.

Day 79. The wild boy is better than color T.V.

Day 86. The wild boy is gone and the face of the pond is dazed by the smile of the moon. It hurts to look there and yet I do

Now that everything is shining.

Skyping from Baghdad
March Darin

He called her "Mon Cher." In 129 emails, seven hand-scrawled notes, and three hand-painted cards bearing Monet–like lily pads he had professed his unabashed love for her. Never mind that he was 6,000 miles away in Baghdad fixing bombed-out schools and she was in Chicago mending her daughter's heart left jagged by a smirking high school quarterback.

His heartfelt missive in all caps accompanied the latest floral offering ordered through bouquet.com. "Tu es une femme la plus remarquable qui est mon amie la plus chere." When he said he had translation help, she imagined some paunchy French national patiently enunciating his prose d' amour in a cement–block bunker. "Geez, no," he laughed through her cell. "I use the Internet translation sites."

Not quite the dramatic scene she had envisioned. No matter. The next day she strategically positioned the blushing pink roses to conceal a hole clawed in her lace tablecloth, the after-effects of a feline brawl.

In last night's, composed at 3 A.M. Baghdad time, (she knew this because he had sent her a time chart for Chicago and Baghdad), he told her that he'd heard birds, an unnatural sound in the city's treeless Green Zone.

"You bring me out of the shadows," he had once written on the tiny card accompanying a desktop heather shrub delivered to her office. She was a balm for the helicopters that woke him every night, their propellers delivering 19-year-old heroes to the main hospital. Some came with limbs as twisted as the licorice their mothers used to pack in their lunchboxes.

Like a love-sick suitor trying to beat out Rhett Butler for his Scarlett, he lavished her with gifts. Milk chocolate from England, jewelry of muted garnet and other stones native to ancient Mesopotamia. Stones she should feel free to sell if it ever got that bad, he said.

He even deposited $3,000 in her bank account, an emergency fund more promising than the green plastic jar of coins she kept on the kitchen counter. For her future security, he paid for a fancy resume package so she could get a better job. Maybe even break into government.

For her mind, he sent her a baby blue mini-laptop so compact it fit snugly in her tote bag. For her spirit, he sent a guide to Illinois birds abd Joni Mitchell's *Ladies of the Canyon*. She remembered when they'd listened to "Yellow Taxi" (in vinyl) in her dorm room as freshmen. He had come to the small Michigan college from Cleveland, saving up for his own ticket on Amtrak when his father told him college was a waste. He had worked side by side with his dad rolling steel. For much of his childhood, his mom had drifted in and out of psyche wards. She had electro-shock therapy, which stole her mind slowly like a kid emptying a jar of penny candy. Yet Mike, who had been through so much, could still laugh at Mel Brooks.

He confessed that he had fallen in love with her then, but was too shy to let her know. She had ended up marrying one of his best friends. Thumbing through an alumni magazine (the "Transitions" column), he discovered she was divorced. His soul-wrenching regret was transformed into boldness. He began attending engineering conferences in Chicago, showing up at her place to cook spaghetti or take her to out to dinner. He had salt and pepper hair, and a kind smile almost making him look young again in his black-framed glasses.

When contracting business dried up in Florida last fall, he had gone to Baghdad, lured by the inflated salaries given in compensation for the threat of living with IEDs.

They each had three children. He, however, had something else—a wife. "She...we have no life together, Mon Cher," he explained. "She does not understand me."

Still, she explained that she could not cross the boundary of physical intimacy. "I will not disrespect your wife, your kids, or my kids," she wrote him plainly. Her true feelings were a mystery to her.

The mini laptop that arrived from Amazon had a built-in web cam, a tiny hole at the top of her screen that burned like Venus when they skyped together. Skype... she liked how it sounded illicit. She saw him in his Baghdad room, his brown eyes little slits at 6 A.M. while she was just getting ready to watch Anderson Cooper on CNN. He told her about the waste of government dollars that could feed every unemployed auto worker in Detroit. The graveyard of Humvees and tanks that lay unattended because the Iraqis had no concept of maintenance. The 19 soldiers who'd died taking showers because of faulty wiring. The wizened faces of tortured Iraqis tortured by those now guarding their compound in the International Zone.

His next assignment was to rebuild a waste treatment plant that lay abandoned because there was no maintenance plan. There was honor, he said, maybe even redemption, in rebuilding the country that we had destroyed.

In turn, she told him about her week—the small triumphs and dramas that filled her days. On Saturday she had taken her daughter to a hip Wicker Park tattoo parlor to get her navel pierced. Her son had landed a job at Game Stop, selling the techno toys he never stopped playing behind closed doors. Sometimes she talked about her work at a non-profit where she was a professional beggar, convincing foundations to unleash dollars for her community mental health clinic. He remembered how at college she had pursued him out of the cafeteria, insisting he sign a petition banning non-union lettuce.

Suddenly his emails became more urgent. Sometimes at midnight she would sit by the glare of her 10-inch computer screen, clicking her inbox to discover unread messages that began, "Mon Cher, it is midnight, are you online? She felt as if she were being stalked, however benignly, by a man 6,000 miles away...

He wrote that he'd be stateside for his daughter's graduation in California, flying back to Baghdad via Chicago. Would she see him again? He was pleading. He'd respect her boundaries and be content to embrace on Michigan Avenue, if only for a few minutes. If only she would. Nothing in California could deter him. She could not resist his persistent offer, demand, really. Her reserve was melting like brown sugar and butter on the stove. What did he write about living in the now? Even that famous historian who put John Adams on the bestseller list had said that the past and future do not exist—only the vicissitudes of the present.

His flight was due in on June 14 at 3 P.M. "I don't want to put you out," he protested when she offered to pick him up at O'Hare. He would grab a taxi, and whisk her away to a trendy Italian place in the city. Her kids were with their dad for the next two days. She washed out the French press, remembering he liked his coffee strong.

To quell her hunger, she made herself a grilled cheese sandwich. She watered and misted her plants, even the Boston fern by the fireplace that burned chemical logs. She switched on the TV, not her usual practice but it calmed her. Simon Cowell smirked at the evening's final contestant on *American Idol*, sending the Prince Wannabe off the charts forever. Later, Anderson Cooper reported that an IED had exploded in a Baghdad alley, dismembering an Iraqi widow and five children. Later still, Conan O'Brien was finally silent.

She pressed the button turning off the TV screen and groped along her overstuffed couch toward a small oak table. She tapped a button, and her little computer screen flickered, emitting the room's only light. After a deep breath she logged off, closed the laptop, and sat alone in the darkness.

Transformation

John Dreyer

Sun grows dark, moon runs blood,
green-tailed meteors scorch the sky.

Out of bubbling abyss, psyche's dark backwaters,
roars One-Eyed-Jack and his band of laments,
his vertigos of regrets, his jokers wild.

Purple orb pulses above prickly pear nose
on hellfire-ringed face; gangrenous tongue
twitches and darts, slithery, viperish.

Round his neck a bloody red flag,
his *jolie rouge*, no quarter today,
and none tomorrow.

Breath toxic as coal tar, timbre molten as lava,
he fires hollow-tipped words, venom-dipped dum-dums:
death to egos and ids.

Sure, sticks and stones can break your bones
but One-Eyed-Jacks can rip your heart out,
strip your soul down, transform you:

now, you're no one.

The Underachiever
Eve Edelson

Anyone can say he's a vampire. People claim to be all sorts of things. She met hers on an autumn night, in a club. The wine played a role, and the weariness, and possibly the pills.

During the final, unsuccessful chemotherapy, she'd given up clubbing. She didn't feel she could carry off the shaved look, and she disliked wigs.

Then one day, trying to hail a cab, she realized she'd become almost invisible. She'd often felt that way at work. The thought, rather than depressing her, produced a tiny burst of energy. Looks no longer mattered. That evening, after taking her pills, she threw on one of her few remaining dresses. She had been so pleased to get down to her college weight.

The club was dingy and the wine, slow in coming, arrived with a dirty glass. She wondered why, with death staring her in the face, or at least peering round the corner, she could not bring herself to make a fuss. When she looked up again, the stranger stood before her.

"May I join you?" he asked.

He had a nice face. Points off for extremely out-of-date clothing—the seventies had not been kind to men's fashion—but noticing that she existed was in his favor. That, and not mentioning the vampire business. She would not have asked him to sit if he had mentioned that. She didn't believe in vampires, or in the mental health of people who thought themselves vampires.

He began, shyly, to ask her about herself, and seemed genuinely interested in her indifferent career in museum curation. Stalled in a field more competitive than sports, she had plunged grimly into a doctoral program in folklore. While the other students waited for their advisors to die, and she labored on the topic her advisor favored—"Images of the Supernatural in European Folk Art"—the symptoms began. Sweating, weakness, lumps.

She knew what vampires were supposed to be. Any creep could go around biting people. That and two bucks would get you on the bus.

The stranger asked about her family (none) — friends (few) — what music she liked (he liked the same kind). He did not ask about her hair. Halfway through the wine, she laughed. She kept meaning to ask him about himself. He left the wine alone.

Eventually, the stranger pulled her chair back for her, held her sweater, held the door. As they emerged into the alley, a rat skittered past. She gasped, stumbled into the stranger's arms and found herself staring up into his dark eyes, which followed the rat with apparent regret as it disappeared behind a dumpster. When she shivered, he draped his jacket around her.

"You're so thin," he said, not seeming put off. He leaned over, framed in moonlight, brow furrowed as if he were trying to remember how to kiss, or nerving himself up to do it. Then he did kiss her.

There was no spark, not even a little one between the shoulder blades. His lips felt like cold rubber.

"How about your place," he said. "Mine's a mess."

The doctors had been honest. There was no point waiting for warm lips to come along.

As they walked, he kept a courtly hand on her arm. A dog fled on sight, cats sprang for fire escapes, and a few seedy-looking characters turned aside into the shadows.

At her door, she remembered her apartment was empty.

She'd wanted to spare the landlord trouble. Clothing had gone to Goodwill. Furniture—and the cruel mirror—to the sidewalk. Important papers trashed unshredded. The dissertation took flight from the roof, introduction going west, bibliography east. She felt lighter. Her Will left what she'd managed to put aside to her alma mater, which had given her a good start in life. The sleeping bag stayed.

She'd seen enough needles and pills, and knew little of guns. The plan that took shape involved a long walk into the woods, and as much wine as she could carry. She would grow ever lighter, become light itself, and take flight with the last of the leaves. The nights grew longer and cooler. The hospice people stopped calling. She liked the emptiness, forgot it might seem strange.

Now her guest hesitated in the doorway. She drew him inside and there saw just how pale he was.

She returned from the kitchen with beers, to find him circling the empty living room as if measuring it. "Minimal," he said. "Interesting."

He spiralled in toward her. The wine and walking had taken their toll. She swayed against his chest, listened, listened harder, drew back and looked at him. He nuzzled her neck, did a walkthrough inspection with his tongue, and bit her.

She'd been through a lot in the hospital. Some people know how to draw blood, others don't. She had thought she knew pain. The ceiling danced. Then she was free, and he was wiping his mouth.

"Sorry," he said. He did look sorry, and surprised, and proud. "Your veins really stand out."

Had she heard him right? He stood between her and the door, in his ridiculously loud shirt, striped pants, zipped boots.

"Who taught you to kiss? Are you a vampire?"

She meant it as sarcasm.

"I don't like to bring that up first thing," he said.

He backed away as her expression changed. Indignation trumping panic, she tottered forward and punched him. Her hand hurt. She didn't care. It was one thing to be made of light, another to be made light of.

"Breathe," she demanded.

He produced a few mechanical huffs. "I'm out of practice."

She grabbed, then abandoned his wrist, pressed ungentle fingers to his neck, stamped in frustration. "You're not a vampire, you're not." Stamping hurt. Being in her skin hurt. "You're a twisted moron who bites people."

"Girls," he said. "Women," he added hastily. "Sometimes." He shrank under her glare, even as her legs wobbled.

They sat on the floor, six-pack between them. She got through the first beer quickly, and kept the bottle at the ready. Let him try something. "How old are you?" she asked.

Was that hesitation? Were wannabe vampires vain?

"I'm two hundred and fifty. Almost." The calculation seemed to tax him. Perhaps one could be a vampire *and* a moron.

"Where's your castle?"

"Not everyone has a castle and three girlfriends." The bitterness was evident. "Though I have some photos that might impress you. Intimate ones."

"Dirty pictures," she said. "A freak who bites people, and collects dirty pictures."

"*Cultured.* Heard of Sarah Bernhardt?"

She took another beer. "Details." Let him try.

"Nineteen thirteen," he said, easily. "Paris. To show off to her friends." He was sitting up straighter. "I went to her dressing room, merely to pay my respects. People might find her over the top now, but in those days she seemed extraordinary."

"Stop. You sat in a theater and watched Sarah Bernhardt?"

"Did you think I hung from the rafters?" said the possible vampire. "I had a ticket. I took it off some oaf who couldn't have appreciated her. Fifth row center, a thousand beating hearts wrapped in silk and velvet, and all I saw was her. Up close, without the make-up, it was another matter. Still, when she made her proposition, I didn't think twice."

"Did she know you were—" It was impossible to say the absurd thing.

"It suited her splendidly. She slept all day." He sighed. "Those were the nights. Regular blood, nothing required of me." He caught her look. "Please," he said. "I mean nothing. She was ancient. Anyway, she wasn't interested in becoming—like me. I only had to squire her around and look good. Well I *do*—you kissed me."

She thought of telling him how his lips had tasted, then lost her patience with the beer. The stranger reached over and opened the bottle for her, gallantly ignoring her flinch. "Is she in the photos *with* you?" she demanded.

"We're in togas. It was artistic."

She was unable to hold back a snicker.

"Whatever," he said, slouching. "Do you want to see or not?"

At that hour there were no cabs. The stranger slowed to match her pace. Finally they halted before a boarded-up building. It was a bad area, but the thought of making her way back, alone, was now beyond her. The wine's headache had begun its distant drum-beat. The rank stairwell seemed endless until it ended at a dark doorway, where she halted, panting.

"I invite you in," he said, making no move to turn on the lights. Gradually her eyes adjusted.

Things, things everywhere, on top of and under and around other shabby things. Feeble moonlight through one draped window outlined piles of magazines, bags of clothing, bags of bags, cobwebbed appliances, empty bottles, a stringless guitar, a table topped with a bowl of mummified fruit. The dust raised by their entrance danced in the thick air.

She regretted her audible sniff. "I don't entertain much," said her host, shifting from foot to foot. She shook off a sting of pity. She sank onto a shaky chair while her host rooted through a dresser drawer stuck halfway open. He placed an old photo album before her. "See? Togas."

She realized she had no idea what Sarah Bernhardt had looked like. As she turned the fragile pages, her host watched expectantly.

"You did not know Teddy Roosevelt," she said finally, in a small voice. "Or Sitting Bull. Or any of those people." She shut the album. "Big deal. Reality is a crutch for people without Photoshop."

He looked blank.

"You faked it," she said. "On a computer?"

"I keep meaning to get one of those."

"Two hundred and fifty," she said. "Years. Old." She hadn't meant it to sound like a character deficiency.

"I do want to improve myself," said her host. "Always something new coming down the pike. Like electricity. I knew then, things were changing, and a fellow had to keep up. I thought of applying to trade school just the other year—oh—1980. Guess I missed the deadline."

The year the principal had told her she could accomplish anything if she tried.

"I suppose money's no problem," she said doubtfully, looking at the squalor. "You must have put aside enough for years of rainy days."

He hung his head.

"Is it like this for all of you? Do you all just bog down?" she asked.

"No," he said at last. "Just me."

She searched for encouraging words. "What had you thought of studying?"

"Bartending. Something to do at night."

She bit her lip.

"The Internet," he said. "Have you tried it?"

Did he even have electricity? "I could help you with computers, and things," she said, mentally re-arranging furniture. "Have you thought of fixing the place up?"

He would think her pushy.

"Could you? Help with stuff?" he asked.

Worse. He looked eager. Would he be grateful? Should it matter? The headache had formally announced itself with a stab over her left eye.

"Look," she said, "you seem nice. Go out, meet people."

Her host brightened. "I met you," he said.

A smile bubbled up inside her. "Did you plan to bite me all along?" she asked. "Honestly."

"Really not. I don't know what came over me."

"Come on. You're a vampire." She'd said it. She'd gone off the deep end.

"I don't prefer girls. Women." He was gay. It figured.

"Or men. Anything that talks," said the man who she now couldn't help thinking of as a vampire. "It's a weakness." He cradled the photo album. "I'm not good about time," he said. "It just goes. There's always tomorrow."

Her smile re-submerged, and a mean flower of resentment bloomed in her gut. This man who could never die, who had outlasted the Revolution, the War of 1812, the Mexican War, the Civil War, the Spanish War, the War to End All Wars and all the wars after that, had never finished a thing he'd started.

"I have six months," she said. "Maybe."

Her fists clenched, unbidden. He was smelling her. "I thought you were just pale," he said. "Or a junkie." She crossed her arms.

"The hair, that's not a punk thing, then," he said. "Punk is so over. I knew that."

She didn't want pity anyway.

"I can give you more time," he said.

"How much?" She was half-listening. The headache had hit its stride, nausea bringing up the rear.

"Forever. Unless you get killed—could happen to anybody."

It was time to leave. The door was so far away.

"You'll have time for everything," he said.

"At night," she replied, fishing for her pills and forming a clear picture of where she'd left them, on her kitchen counter.

"There are drawbacks," he said. "Still, it's not a bad offer... considering."

"Considering what?"

"Considering you're, like, dying, and considering I don't even want to bite you."

"You *did* bite me."

"I didn't enjoy it. But now I'm sorry for you."

Pity. Damn.

"Don't think too long," said the vampire. "I'm a rolling stone." As he leaned back, dust rose around him.

"Where do you get it?" she asked, and he understood.

"Rats. And the butcher." He answered more unasked questions. "Some people can turn into mist and whatnot. I never got the hang of it. Staking just hurts, a lot. Sunlight, bad. That's written in stone."

A course in English composition would do him no harm.

"Otherwise you pretty much go on forever, if someone doesn't cut your head off. But how often does that happen?"

"Would it hurt?" she asked, and he understood.

"Not unless you clot. Which you aren't doing so well." He touched her neck, and she did not shrink. "I'm not coming on to you." Of course he wasn't. She knew what she looked like.

Rats. Butcher shops.

No more pain.

"Can any vampire do it for me?" she asked delicately, hoping to preserve her options. She'd offended him.

"I suppose you'd prefer Dracula," he said, looking away.

She was so tired. "Would I look like this? Forever?"

"Like how?" asked her vampire.

"Like a hag."

He looked her up and down and said, without art, "What do you mean? You look fine."

Despite having managed, momentarily, to make immortality seem unattractive, he was sort of sweet.

"It's a big step," she said.

But she had decided. She wondered how he had come to be what he was, but they could go into that later. So much needed doing. She could clean this dump for a start. Do something about his clothes. Get him into night school. A man could change.

All the King's Men

Robert Klein Engler

Dried oak leaves litter the ground at Austin
Gardens in Oak Park. A few tulips poke through,
fingering their way to early March sunlight.

They say the Sibyl of ancient Rome wrote her
prophecies on oak leaves, and then the wind
scattered them, so her message was part here

and part there, like the leaves I see at my feet,
a mystery going to mold, the future foretold
but unclear about what follows in the puzzle,

or why the police found the body of Rafael
Ramirez, dismembered and in four garbage
bags behind a garage in an Oak Park alley

while children tease, "Humpty Dumpty sat
on a wall. Humpty Dumpty had a great fall."

I know you're burdened and world weary.
You dream of a place by the sea where waves
wash in with the soft lull of a warm breeze.

There, you let desire dissipate, and like love
that finds what it seeks, you rest; speechless,
steady, enduring like the oak of prophecy

or photos that show Rafael's skin was the soft
color of oak leaves and the police say his body
was left randomly in Oak Park the way wind

scatters randomly the leaves of Austin Gardens
and dark scratches of the Sybille in her prophecy
telling us in rhyme of the barbarians to come,

when all the king's horses and all the king's
men couldn't put Rafael together again.

Mango Rash

Gretchen Fletcher

Would Eve have eaten this fruit
I pick now in the Eden of my yard? Dared
to take it to her kitchen and with a paring knife
strip away skin, revealing flesh
the color of all the suns that rose
and set while it hung, green and hard, waiting?
If some fork-tongued, scaly reptile had told her
it would cause a pleasurable pain,
would she have thought him a liar? How
could she have believed
such an exquisite itch—

remembered from my youth
when I dared to eat a mango whole
down to its big, hairy seed and let its juice run
down my flat-nippled, child's chest—
the next day broken out
in tiny pustules that spread knowledge
with their poison fire when scratched—

remembered now
as I peel this one under
running water to lessen the risk,
knowing full well I might
still have to pay the price.

⋮

70

⋮

Bigfoot in the Backyard
Gail Folkins

On a mountain hike with Mom, a branch falls—I jump. Between dense trees and my imagination, it's easy to get lost up here. I follow the path and wave a stick to catch the spider webs in front of us. Our dog, Buffy, weaves under ferns and hops over the logs my brother threw across the trail to keep out motorbikes, trespassers, maybe Bigfoot. It makes the path harder to find; Ken says it's just in case.

We walk by huckleberries bursting pink from logs, while evergreens lean in breezes too tall for me, at age 11, to feel. I hear the underbrush crunch, a squirrel looking for berries. Mom and I create our own share of crackling when we lose the trail and stumble into ferns and purple bleeding hearts. My jeans are wet with raindrops.

At the edge of the second creek, something crashes. The crumpled ferns could mean a bear; my legs freeze and breathing can wait. Mom stops in the marshy part of the creek. She's not big anyway, and looks smaller as she listens. I can tell from her eyes she's on the edge of being afraid, if not already there.

Bigfoot, my mind says. Sasquatch, his Native American name, matches the sound he's making. He's the one thrashing in the fir trees and smashing ferns. He'd been in the news so much, it had to be. My brother and I read every Bigfoot sighting or report, never mind that most appeared in the back of the daily paper or in sections like Northwest Living. We'd pass news stories and pictures of murder victims, young women in their late teens and twenties with long, straight hair. Their smiles, captured in high school photos, floated across the pages. My stick-straight hair looked a little like theirs.

"Let's go back," Mom says. Her face is calm, but the pace she sets, a dead run, isn't. I drop my spider stick and tear past the webs that grab me, not daring to look behind us. We spot the bridge over the first creek, the place I thought we'd slow down. Mom pounds her boots across it and charges up the hill. Past the edge of the woods, she walks the last steps into our yard. I take a few breaths and wait for my heart to catch up.

The familiar setting, wild with spring roses and honeysuckle, makes Sasquatch harder to swallow. Even Buffy, now begging for a treat, looks as if she's forgotten. I kick the dirt with my tennis shoe. When I look up, my brother's leaning against a tree. Thick dark curls, the opposite of my light brown tangles, frame his face. Five years older than me, Ken dresses in browns and greens to match the forest. He knows deer, bear, and the great-horned owls with their swiveling heads. He stares at me, waiting to hear why we'd run home.

I want Mom to tell him; he'll believe her more than me. She moves away from the trail's end to the damp earth and doesn't say anything. After poking some yellow blooms near a fallen log, she starts to weed. "Whatever it was, it was loud," she says. She calls to one of the cats. "Skipper, where have you been?"

With Mom talking to the orange tabby, I know it's up to me. My words, too eager, spill out. "It was big, really big. It crashed through the woods, louder than anything."

Ken leans from the honeysuckle-covered tree and reacts as he does to all little-sister news. "It was probably a deer." The smirk on his face steadies.

I scowl hard. "No, it was louder."

"A bear, maybe."

Not wanting the others to see I'm afraid, I stop talking about it. Mom, still busy with the dirt, keeps quiet. I search her face for clues, but the woman who ran down the mountain has gone someplace else. The emotions we won't speak stay hidden for now, back in the forest where Bigfoot lives.

———

Another Pacific Northwest mother fidgets in front of the sink and watches the coming rain. The worry she won't name is her son, Ted. She's watched him grow up, first in Pennsylvania and now in Washington. She told him she was his sister—because she was unmarried, it seemed best. Her parents, really his grandparents, became Ted's parents, too. His real father in Philadelphia was never a part of his life.

When she and Ted moved to Washington, joining distant relatives in Tacoma, Ted had a hard time leaving the comfort of his grandparents, though she soon met a man in Tacoma and married. She hoped her son would get along with her new husband; though the couple did their best to raise him, Ted remained standoffish to his stepfather.

The woman looked down at her soapy hands. She never told her son the truth about being his mother—Ann Rule, author of *The Stranger*

Beside Me, says he called her "Louise," and sometimes "Mother." Ever since he'd made a trip back east to meet with the rest of the family, it was as if he knew, though he never discussed it with her.

Now that he's planning on studying law, she hopes things will improve. Maybe he'll develop a good career and find a nice girl to marry. Things didn't work out with his first girlfriend, but given his good looks and book smarts, he'll attract someone else soon enough. Maybe there'll even come a time someday soon when his eyes lose their contempt, a resentment that breaks her heart every time.

I try to forget Bigfoot after our run down the mountain, but my brother won't let me. "There's a Bigfoot movie on TV," he tells me one night, leaning across the beige Formica countertop. Mom, plaid fabric all around her, sews a new shirt in the living room. Dad stays in the bedroom looking at the designs he brings home from work.

"I'm reading," I say, even though Ken's comment is more command than question. I bury my face in the nearest book.

"Whatsamatter, you scared?" My brother's lips poise to grin.

"No, I've just seen those shows already." I don't want to see the new film clip again, the one where Bigfoot lopes into a clearing before escaping into the screen's fuzzy edges. His stride looks purposeful, unafraid. The tape has no sound, so I can't tell if his steps match the ones we heard in the woods.

Ken's program could be a tamer nature show where scientists debate the real and the fake. During one of these specials, a man shows a 20-inch footprint mold that someone built as a hoax. Their fakeness doesn't make me feel any better, the crashing I'd heard that day real as ever.

"It's a new movie," Ken says, stretching an arm toward the television. He flicks the channel and smiles, probably because he gets to watch a movie and scare me at the same time.

From my spot at the kitchen table, I tug my blue sweatshirt sleeves around my hands and hug my knees, more willing to face my own fear than Ken's scorn. At the opening credits, I debate whether to close the kitchen curtains. With the drapes open, we'd have enough time to spot Bigfoot. Closing them shut out the night, and also meant he could sneak up on us. "What about the curtains?" I ask.

Ken's thick eyebrows align in disapproval. "Don't worry about it," he says, turning back to the television screen.

I only half-watch the Bigfoot movie. When the music grows loud, I stare at the pages of my book. This made-for-TV-movie doesn't have as much to do with Bigfoot as Ken hoped; he sits through it anyway, too stubborn to try another show. When the ending credits trail down the screen, we both turn away from the television news. Ken thinks it's boring. I roll my eyes and feign agreement.

The truth is I don't want to hear their grim, real-life stories. Before I can run to the fridge for a Sprite, I might catch an update on another slender, straight-haired woman in the Seattle area who's disappeared, a clean-cut man named Ted the prime suspect. Most of his victims part their hair down the middle. I part mine on the side, I tell myself.

The pop can's beaded sides cool my hand. My brother searches for another show to watch. Mom comes into the kitchen to see what we're up to; even though it's the weekend, I'm ready for bed. I go to my room and pull on pajamas. Like a turned channel, my thoughts snap back to Bigfoot. A half-hour later and still awake, I'm happy my brother's room is right beside mine; glad he's not going to college for a few more years.

⎯⎯⎯⎯⎯⎯

At dawn, in a home close to the University of Washington, an alarm goes off that no one answers. Normally, 21-year-old Lynda Healy wakes up around 5:30 a.m. to work at a radio station just a few blocks down the street. After work, Lynda studies and spends time with her friends and roommates. One roommate hears the alarm that won't stop; she goes into Lynda's room, but the bed is made up and the room empty. Her roommate assumes she's gone to work.

Lynda's family members, who live on the east side of Lake Washington, come for a dinner she's promised to cook them that night. Their daughter, who never arrived at work, doesn't show. Her parents question the roommates, none of whom have seen her, and call the Seattle police. Lynda isn't the type to miss work or class, let alone a family dinner. At first, police find Lynda's bed made and room clean, just as her roommate has. Moments later, they'll find a missing outfit. They'll also discover the bed isn't made as Lynda would have, and a pillow stained with blood.

⎯⎯⎯⎯⎯⎯

I wrestle my sheets and pull them closer to my chin. Footsteps echo on the deck outside my window. My eyes crack open to the noise. It's light out, barely. I think of last night's movie and curl my toes tighter. The deck around our house didn't always reach past my window. Dad added on to the house this summer, making the new deck wrap around it like gift ribbon. I watched, helpless, while Dad gave his project every weekend moment until dark-colored boards marched down the house. "Maybe you could just build it partway," I'd say.

Dad took a break from his nailing and looked up at me. "It'll look better down the whole side." Narrow boards spread out beneath his arms.

As promised, the new deck blends into the old version as if they're the same. No matter how good it looks, I can't get used to it. Most nights I lie awake in bed, listening for heavy footsteps on fresh-painted wood. To me, its long timbers are an open invitation to Bigfoot, who'd stomp along its length and stare inside the windows.

Burying myself back in the sheets, I roll away from the window. A new deck means worse things than Bigfoot. On the edge of adolescence, I sense other disadvantages, such as curious parents or my brother and his friends peering into my window. I grasp the covers tighter. Other intruders, those I don't know at all, can just as easily stare inside. Like the stranger named Ted, who some claim to have seen at the old barn where I take horseback riding lessons. I try to forget my friends' whispers about this good-looking man, the one who makes young women disappear.

Twenty-three-year-old Janice Ott, eager to get into the water, hastens her steps to Lake Sammamish State Park, located east of Seattle. Fierce sunshine, rare even in the warmest Pacific Northwest summers, flickers against the lake. Janice lays down her bike, which she's ridden from her home in downtown Issaquah, and settles onto the grass for some sun.

On this Sunday afternoon, the park is crowded with people taking advantage of the weather. One of them, a single man in shorts and a shirt, walks up to the spot where Janice suns herself. Janice sees the man with his arm in a sling standing over her. She can't place him—maybe a friend of her husband.

"Could you help me with my sailboat?" the man says. He's good looking, with light-brown hair and a slight smile. "I can't load it onto the car with this arm." He points to a Volkswagen Beetle with a ski rack, parked in the trees.

Janice waits before answering. She's sure she doesn't recognize this man, but it wouldn't hurt to help. "Sure," she says. "But I don't want to leave my bike."

"You can put it on top of my car," he says. "I'll drive you back."

Janice picks up her bike and starts walking alongside the man.

He returns the smile and matches her steps. Other witnesses watch the two chatting together as they leave. The sun lengthens its reach. Janice and the man walk further away from the shining lake and into the trees, closer to the VW, no sailboat, and darkness.

———·———

In the woods behind our house, an overhead branch snaps. I don't jump. Buffy bounds over a log that's ahead of me. Clouds make a ceiling over alders, already bare, while the still-lush Douglas firs wave their branches. Months after our run down the mountain, I don't mind walking on the path by myself; Bigfoot and I can share. Spider stick in hand, I choose my steps and smell the coming rain.

On a trail thick with ferns and songbirds, it's easier to embrace mythic creatures and ignore realities, like a serial killer who prowls western Washington and later, beyond. The headlines I gloss over in search of Sasquatch name Ted Bundy, who assaults several Seattle women during the 1970s. In 1974, he travels east of Seattle to the Cascade foothills. Using looks, charm, and a fake cast to make him seem helpless, he kills two women at Lake Sammamish, a park just below our mountain. Both his victims are slim, both have straight hair. Janice Ott and I share the same hometown.

Looking up, I touch a gold vine maple leaf, a sign summer's turning to fall. A last grove of bleeding hearts fades nearby. Though I've made my peace with Bigfoot, I'm not ready for more sinister monsters, the everyday kind tougher to spot on walks through gentle streams and huckleberry bushes. I point my spider stick a step or two ahead, just enough to see what I know: the trail, the rain, my brother's logs. Under the sway of Douglas firs, Sasquatch blends softer with the forest and its whispers. Buffy beside me, I scan the trees and listen.

A Dinner Disturbed

Peter Goodwin

She sat at the table next to mine and disturbed my dinner—
she and her breasts shimmering in the candle light
two perfect orbs displayed
floating, proclaiming, boasting
teasing, enticing, taunting.
Food I had thought delicious
now seemed boring, tasteless and flat.
I willed myself to concentrate on my dinner
eyes down, fork in hand
but fork and finger became clumsy
and my eyes drifted sideways
unable and unwilling to resist those inviting, brazen breasts
breasts firm and flexible, skin soft and smooth
two delicious pots of honey, and every male wants a taste.
Waiters flutters around like flies at a picnic,
the haughty maitre d' turns himself into an unctuous
groveling suitor offering his services and his business card.
The tone and tension of conversation in the restaurant changes.
The boom and base of men pontificating become distracted,
less certain and women's voices sharper and more assertive
while the subject of all this distraction reflecting in the glory
of her breasts appears serene—apparently indifferent to the rising
        temperature
her smooth, pure unblemished face
her lips in a half smile—just a girl
just another Helen launching a thousand distractions
distorting a thousand dinner conversations
frustrating at least one poet.

⋮

78

⋮

Yard Sale Discovery

Mary Ann Grzych

I really don't have time, I thought. Yet the "Yard Sale Today" arrow beckoned me. *I'll be late for my lunch with Mom. Besides, today is an ambiguous term. The sale could have been yesterday or last week.* I didn't see the usual balloons or flags marking the way, nor any other cars headed down the rather overgrown country lane called Memory. "What a cliché," I said as I pulled off the road, debating whether or not to check it out.

Yard sale treasures fill my tiny campus apartment. They link me to a past I've always longed for, but don't have. I used to fantasize about a childhood where aunts and girl cousins laughed and talked together in a sparkling white kitchen with lace curtains. The smell of Grandma's roast drifts through the house prompting the men to call, "How soon do we eat?" every 10 minutes.

Whenever I asked about relatives, Mom would look down and say they'd all died. No amount of pleading could get her or my dad, who died three years ago, to say anything more.

The horn of an approaching truck startled me from my reverie. I made a u-turn and went back. Something inside me was steering my old Chevy into Memory Lane. I drove slowly down the narrow, dirt road, bumping along under a canopy of huge oaks. Morning sunshine filtering through the trees highlighted white bark curling away from the trunks of river birch interspersed among the oaks.

"What a wild goose chase," I said aloud after going a half mile without seeing a house, another car, or anything except trees and gathering gloom. Branches brushed the car's roof, the air felt stifling, yet a phantom voice inside urged me on. I eased the car around a final bend in the road and emerged into bright sunshine. A cool breeze tousled my naturally curly black hair and I could breathe again. Bright red letters spelled out "Yard Sale" on the drive leading to a neat, white clapboard farmhouse at the end of the road. A smile lifted the corners of my mouth when I saw no other cars around; I'd have my pick of the items for sale in the front yard.

The lawn was freshly cut as I stepped out and paused to savor the smell of ripening apples. It was eerily quiet. Tables full of multi-color Melmac dishes from the fifties, aprons, towels, canning jars and kitchen gadgets didn't interest me; nor did the chenille bedspreads, which might have, if they hadn't been so worn and discolored. I was beginning to think that this was time wasted after all, when I saw a small bedside table—perfect for the maple Jenny Lind bed I'd slept in all my life. A yellowed tag on the drawer pull said $10. I couldn't resist and went toward the house to find someone to pay. A few steps away I noticed a small table holding a flat, grey metal money box with a sign: "Please leave the money for your purchase here."

Rummaging through my purse, I found three singles and a twenty. "Damn." Not sure I wanted to pay twenty, and not expecting to find anything but an empty box, I raised its lid. Inside was a single ten dollar bill. *This day is getting stranger by the minute.* I put my crisp twenty in and took the worn, wrinkled ten.

After placing the table in the Chevy's trunk, an overwhelming curiosity engulfed me. Why wasn't anyone around to oversee such a large yard sale? Almost before I realized what was happening, I found myself climbing the stairs to the porch.

I sensed, before I stepped on it, that the third step would creak. When it did, an icy arrow shot up my spine freezing me in place. Reaching for the railing, I hung on with both hands like a toddler just learning to navigate steps. The railing was warm—comforting under my hand, and the chill left me, but not the feeling that something weird was happening.

The porch was empty, but I felt there should be brown wicker chairs and a rocking horse with a bright red saddle. My head told me to leave. Now! Yet a compulsion stronger than fear forced my hand to the knocker.

"Hello, anyone there?" Nothing.

Shielding my eyes, I pressed against the screen squinting at the empty interior; then eased the unlocked door open and stepped inside. Unlike the clean, well kept exterior of the house, the inside was dark, neglected and foreboding. Floral wallpaper, yellowed with age, was peeling from the walls of what must have been a large parlor. An old, green leaf patterned rug had a threadbare spot in front of two deep depressions that could only have been made by a rocking chair. *Someone must have sat there rocking back and forth for hours, dragging their feet on the carpet.* I shuddered at the image, but my obsession with the house overcame the instinct to flee.

In the kitchen, white, wooden cabinets hung above a yellow Formica counter. Two empty cabinets, their doors hanging askew on broken hinges, flanked a rusty sink. Tattered lace curtains still hung on the windows. Trembling, I envisioned a maple high chair next to a round oak table. The smell of roast beef filled the room. I wanted to escape, but couldn't move. I wanted to scream, but no sound came from my dry throat. I heard the echo of women's laughter and men calling, "When do we eat?" Legs shaking, I reached for the table that wasn't there. Sweat ran down my face and my heart began turning back-flips as I fled from the house and the memories, if that's what they were. The screen door's slam echoed in the stillness behind me.

At the edge of the lawn, I paused, gasping, to look back. The house and tables appeared as they had before—well organized and inviting. I drove recklessly back down Memory Lane unable to shake the feeling that I was leaving part of myself behind.

My heart rate and breathing had calmed long before I pulled into Mom's driveway two hours later, yet the phantom voice inside told me I'd go back to Memory Lane—soon.

"Where'd you get that?" Mom asked, holding the door to her Chicago bungalow open as I carried the table inside.

"It's a strange story," I replied, setting the table down in the parlor. "I'll tell you later. I smell spaghetti sauce and I'm starved."

After lunch, Mom insisted we take our coffee into the parlor. "Tell me that strange story," she said. I had barely begun when she stopped me.

"What was the road called?"

"Memory Lane."

"You're sure?" her voice quivered slightly.

"Who could forget a name like that?"

I related the story, skipping my experience inside the house. Something told me not to tell Mom about that. When I finished, she was pale; her cup rattled, spilling coffee into the saucer as she set it down. "Are you OK?" I asked, reaching out to touch her hand. It felt unnaturally cold.

"Fine, just a little tired," she assured me. "Let's see that table." Her straight blonde hair fell across her shoulders as she leaned forward.

"I was in such a hurry I didn't really examine it," I said opening the table's drawer to discover a tarnished silver picture frame holding a 5"x7", black and white photograph of a smiling, dark haired woman in a rocker, with a toddler on her lap wearing a white pinafore and a locket. A handsome, curly haired man stood beside them, his hand resting on the woman's shoulder.

"Look," I exclaimed handing the picture to Mom. "This must be the family that lived there."

She gasped, turned ashen, and fell back onto the couch. The picture clattered to the floor shattering the glass." Mom, what's wrong?" I cried. She couldn't speak. When the ambulance arrived she was unconscious, but still breathing.

———†———

I paced the hospital waiting room, arms folded tightly across my chest; fingers kneading my biceps. Finally, the doctor came out.

"Your mother's had a severe heart attack," he said, leading me to a private corner of the waiting room. "She's stable now, but the next 24 hours are crucial."

"You're telling me," I choked on the words, "she could die?"

"I wish I could be more positive," he replied gently. "But you need to be prepared."

"Can I see her?" I asked, trying to stifle tears pooling in my eyes.

"A nurse will bring you to CICU. You can spend the night with her if you like," he said, retrieving a box of Kleenex from a nearby table.

My night was spent holding Mom's hand, watching the machines even though I hadn't a clue what they meant. At 5 A.M. she woke. Her terrified gaze swept the room, taking in all the machines and tubes attached to her, before fixing on me.

"What happened?" she murmured.

"You had a heart attack," I answered, leaning down to kiss her forehead. "Don't talk. Just rest."

"The picture, I'm sorry," she sighed.

"Don't worry about the picture. It isn't important."

"It is!" she insisted. "The bank vault. It's all there."

One of the machines began to beep rapidly—bringing two nurses on the run. The first nurse leaned over the bed, her stethoscope moving across Mom's chest. "Get the crash cart," she yelled. The loud speaker called, "Code blue," as I stood against the wall, helplessly watching the drama play out before me.

———†———

The day after Mom's funeral, I sat in her kitchen, the safety box's contents spread before me. Her last words, "...it's all there," echoed in my mind. Did she mean the insurance papers, deed to the house, her

Will? All there. Among them was a plain white envelope addressed, "For Molly, after I'm gone." My body tensed as I reached for it. My hands shook and I didn't notice that I'd cut my finger on the flap until a drop of blood stained the paper inside. A heart shaped locket and its chain fell out as I unfolded the paper. It said, simply: My darling Molly, this was yours when you were little. I hope that you will pass it on to your daughter, if you have one. It will be a link to your past. I love you. Mom

Stunned, I sat staring at it for a long time. There was something familiar about the locket, but I couldn't remember wearing it. Why had Mom put it in the safety box? That night, fast asleep in Mom's bed, I dreamt of the farmhouse on Memory Lane. I woke with a start, the image of the bedside table still in my mind. Half asleep I went to the parlor, opened the drawer and took out the picture.

I almost passed the worn, barely legible sign for Memory Lane. Where the road had been just a week ago, there was nothing but scrub brush and three-foot high wild grass. "This can't be!" I exclaimed aloud.

At the house up ahead, I parked and knocked on the front door. A stout, middle aged woman wearing a flowered housedress and apron answered.

"I'm sorry to bother you," I said. "Can you tell me about a farmhouse down at the end of Memory Lane? It's important."

"I'm Mrs. Mueller," she said stepping out onto the porch." That'd be the old Schneider place. Nobody's lived there for 15 years."

"I'm looking for the family that used to live there."

"Oh, that's a sad story. Sit down," she said indicating two blue metal porch chairs.

"Tom and Sarah Schneider lived there with their little girl named Nancy after her grandmother." She sat across from me, her ample figure barely fitting into the chair.

"They had a nice orchard and sold bushels of apples every fall. One September day back in 1983, Sarah put a pie in the oven, then took Nancy down to the apple stand in front of their place. When it was time for the pie to come out, Sarah left Nancy on a stool in the stand and went back to the house. She was only gone a few minutes, but when she came back the child was gone. Sarah searched the yard frantically, then called the police. Policemen with bloodhounds, relatives, and a legion of volunteers searched the woods around the farm for weeks, but that beautiful little girl was never found." She paused, leaned back in her chair and closed her eyes briefly.

"The case was never closed, but the police chief confided to my husband that he was convinced Nancy had been kidnapped. Sarah couldn't forgive herself for leaving her daughter alone those few little minutes. She became so despondent; she couldn't function—just sat in her parlor rocking for hours. One day, around three years later, Tom came in from work to find Sarah dead in the rocker. The doctor said she died of a broken heart."

She paused again, closing her eyes, her forehead furrowed. "Were you close?" I asked, leaning forward. She opened her eyes; looked at me quizzically.

"Yes. You remind me of her. She was about your age; had the same dark hair and deep brown eyes," she replied before continuing.

I pressed back into the chair to distance myself from the story and the suspicion that was growing in my mind. The pain of my nails digging into the palms of my hands brought me back to Mrs. Mueller's voice.

"Tom was a wreck at the funeral—could hardly speak," she said sadly. "Not even Reverend Fowler could make him leave the cemetery after the burial. His parents sat in their car for over an hour watching him curled up on the ground, one arm stretched across Sarah's grave, before he got up and let them take him home.

"The next day his body was found in Sarah's rocker—the gun in his hand. No one in the family wanted anything from that unhappy house. They had a big yard sale, but never sold the house. Over the years the road has grown over."

"Do you know where that family is now?" I asked.

"Sarah's sister sends me a Christmas card. I'll get the address," Mrs. Mueller replied as she went into the house.

Suddenly, there wasn't a whisper of a breeze. I was dizzy, caught in the throes of uncertainty. Had last week's trip down Memory Lane been just a fantasy? If so, where had the table come from? My heart was doing back-flips again.

I didn't wait for the address. Mom's voice saying, "I'm sorry," echoed in my ears as I ran to the car and sped away from what might be the family I'd always yearned for.

Red tailed
Dawnell Harrison

You're a red tailed
Hurricane looking for
A muddy blue tsunami
To compliment your destruction.

Pure as spring water,
Loveless as an abacus,
You smile at your
Accomplishments,
However futile.

You leave a trail
Of dirt, strewn trees,
Roofs, plastic pink flamingos.

Oh, I dream that your
Red tailed hurricane
Is not rapping
At my door
Once again.

non-partners in crime

juley harvey

my soul
and good sense
tell me
to run now,
to leave
the scene
of the not-quite-
accident yet,
while i'm still intact,
before the rubber
and all bridges are burned,
before the paramedics
need to be dispatched,
while i'm still all right,
while you're out of sight.
and here's the thing...
everybody needs a good getaway
driver. yikes.

The Green Box

Nancy J. Heggem

I thought it was in the cupboard.
No, was it under the bed?
I looked in the bread box and lunch box,
the picnic hamper and back pack.

The little girl, such a sweet smile,
with the prepared speech,
how could I resist, indeed, do I ever resist?
It's that time again, not Groundhog Day,
that marks the end of winter.

We leave our houses, even unbutton our coats,
turn our face to the late winter sun.
All would be perfect,
if only I could find the green box,
The Girl Scout Thin Chocolate Mint cookie box.

There Was No Overt Blessing

Deanna Hopper

There was no overt blessing.
The wolf looked at me
With strange light eyes.
He held an embroidered fan.
It was broken, and glistened.
Like all the beautiful things I had ever seen,
A red jewel, a distant castle,
The shell whorl, the forest,
It seemed to promise some other, better, world.
There is no other world, he said.
I was terrified.
As the water rose
He put his arms around me.
The water ran through the house,
Loosening, lifting. As it coursed,
He held my crumbling body.
You see? He said. It is all right.
You have succeeded,
Beyond any dream,
Or melody of a dream.

.

GadZukes

Gary Jugert

It's like having a really bad cold ... this being dead.

You take medicine, you blow your nose a lot, you hope you're getting better, but you still can't breathe, you can't sleep through the night, ooze comes out of places you don't think it should, your mind feels fuzzy, and nobody wants to hang out.

But the flesh eating distinguishes the two.

You might *want* to kill somebody when you have a cold, but I'm more or less obligated. I've tried to steer clear of the roving packs of zombies marching through British towns indiscriminately devouring locals who don't possess effective garden tool head-whacking skills.

So I've moved to Hawaii. I try to stick to a diet of fat poor kids. I've opened up a small ukulele shop.

And which ukulele shop isn't small?

GadZukes ukuleles have become prized possessions of independent musicians all over the internet. A quick search of YouTube reveals my little guitars fuel a nation hungry for a new sound and a simpler way of life. They've turned to the Stradivarius of ukuleles in my GadZukes so often I fear I may become a bit cavalier. The unique finishes I use on my instruments and the tones they produce are so hauntingly beautiful everybody wants a piece of me.

Oddly enough, I'm a bit proud to say not everyone can afford to opt-in on this one.

The stunning treble, the booming base, my attention to every detail of the finish work, and the alluring ghostliness of my ukuleles captures the spirits of musicians and they don't want to put down their GadZukes.

You'll forgive me for smiling while I type. If they only knew what went into the ukuleles, they'd play more minor keys, and sadder songs, and those with moral compasses wouldn't play them at all. Those righteous few will never understand the value of my recycling program, or the charm in having an instrument be the melodious extension of a life cut off too soon.

Don't confuse me with a vampire if I tell you the rest of this story.

You see I use the blood from my dinners to create a deep burgundy finish for my ukuleles. It's a hue you won't find on any other instrument and a bit of DNA testing would go a long way toward proving my creations are far more than simply wood and metal and nylon. I tell everyone about the gut strings, but of course I'm joking. They're nylon. Gut is far too tasty to be saved and strung for music. The blood, on the other hand, isn't my thing.

So gooey and messy.

The vampires stop by here on occasion, using the "Where in the World is the Nearest Paranormal Entity" application on our iPhones, but I turn them away. Even the cute vampires. So many zombies end up married to vampires it's sickening.

"You suck the blood. I'll eat the flesh."

So convenient and symbiotic on paper, but honestly, how long will an immortal be happy with a dead companion? These arrangements inevitably end badly. The vampires stay up too late, they never want to go to lunch, and they're constantly making cameo appearances in badly written novels. Speaking from the zombie perspective, their whole culture is needlessly overdone. We don't have the same maintenance needs.

"There's a person." Chomp.

That's it for us.

No crosses, no dentistry, no cloaks, no coffins, no sexual tension. If you don't behead us with a well aimed hoe, we're all about enjoying a nice meal and the rest of the day we can proceed to be productive citizens. Most of us work in offices in major corporations going from work to home to work. We accept what network television offers us as entertainment. We vote for our favorite American Idol. We think Paris Hilton is interesting.

For me, I bought into the Hawaiian zeitgeist of the ukulele and opened a shop.

Here on the workbench in front of me is my latest instrument. It's a concert size ukulele with a rosewood fret board, gold plated tuning pegs, and a glistening deep red finish. I'm calling it Ernesto. I'm sad to admit I don't know the real name of my breakfast from a few days ago. He was a plump boy with a nice bicycle and probably on his way to school. He didn't have any identification on him. Boys that age never do and so I have to make up names for them. He was a Hawaiian native, so he tasted like the islands. Volcanic, exotic, sweet and spicy. The imported kids from the mainland are better for me, but they're not as tasty.

Ernesto's blood will make this ukulele come to life.

I built this one on special order from a famous player in Chicago. Harpo Giddyup found fame singing a song called, "Take Your Shirt Off If You Love France." The song made him famous, but did not fill up his bank account. Apparently only French men and women disrobed during the song and nobody wanted to pay to see that. When he switched from accordion to ukulele and changed the word France to America he landed a gig on Comedy Central and didn't need to play birthday parties or bar mitzvahs anymore.

He'll love his Ernesto. Too bad I can't tell him who he's really playing.

Ooops, excuse me. There's a knock at the door. That'll be the police.

Okay, back. They seem to be looking for a boy named Aldrich. Now I have to decide if the Ernesto ukulele should become the Aldrich ukulele. Such an ugly name. I think I'll stick with Ernesto. I bet even Aldrich would want it that way. Why do parents name their children such bad names these days? What would be wrong with Robert, or William, or Ronald?

The cops have been by several times since I moved here.

We seem to have a problem in this neighborhood with local kids being snatched by somebody. The police are concerned a slave trader might be working in the area. I like to buy the milk cartons. Sometimes the only way to learn about your dinner is to read the "Have You Seen Me?" section on the milk boxes. I'm hoping to limit the media attention for my culinary escapades to the milk carton portrait gallery. I steer clear of pretty blonde girls in high fashion neighborhoods. The lawyers and doctors who live there tend to become so dramatic when their children go missing. The newspapers, the television, the appearances on Oprah. It's not good for a zombie trying to run a business.

Even when the police stop by to ask questions, they don't stay very long. I'm not the prettiest thing to look at or smell, you know, with the rotting flesh and the poked out eyeball and all this zombie accoutrement. I suppose I could buy a new shirt someday. But my raggedy appearance is why I chose mail order as my principal business. In a world where orders arrive over the phone or by PayPal, even ugly smelly people, even dead people, can eke out a living.

I'm convinced most Ebay-ers are zombies.

I'm also convinced you'd love the tones resonating out of my Ernesto ukulele if you could hear it live, but I need to string it. I'll work on it while we talk.

You'll be able to see the Ernesto on YouTube soon. Harpo Giddyup's audiences love to make cell phone videos of his concerts and load them onto the net. You can imagine the anticipation at every show waiting for "*the* song" and then the pandemonium as audience members desperately pan the room for shirtless fans. The UPS man will stop by this afternoon and the Ernesto, baked, strung, tuned, and packaged will head off to Chicago and infamy.

When people see Harpo playing Ernesto, I'll be flooded with orders and my prices will continue to climb. They'll turn to my website and scroll down the previous projects page and see the Emily, the Andrew, the Lakisha, the Juan. I have seven different Juan's actually.

I went through a naming slump for awhile. Everybody seemed to taste the same. I worried I might be developing Hawaiian intolerance. Zombies have food allergies just like the living and some even turn to eating trolls, and mermaids, and politicians to avoid human flesh. Luckily my stomach problems turned out to be a simple case of too many boys. You don't want to eat too many boys. You can end up with Puppydogtailitis. A balanced diet of eating girls and boys is much better for your soul and your taste buds.

There.

Ernesto is strung up.

Frankly, he feels better in my hands as a finished ukulele than he felt as breakfast food. Of course he'll sound much better now. All that screaming gave me a headache.

Let's start off with a nice F minor chord. I think it's the saddest and scariest chord you can make on a ukulele. I put my index finger on the fourth string's first fret. I put my middle finger onto the second string's first fret. My pinkie reaches out to the third fret on the first string. I'm noticing I need to trim my fingernails again. Why would our hair and fingernails keep growing after death? It doesn't seem right. I couldn't grow hair on my head when I was alive, and now that I'm dead, it keeps flowing out of the back of my skull. I have to cut it myself because the barbers have some rule against helping zombies. Have you ever tried to cut your own hair using a mirror ... and a crooked eyeball?

I strum.

Yes. So sad, so elegant, so haunting.

Aldrich's soul has moved into this charming project and I can hear him haunting the strings. Let's bar the first fret, remove my pinkie and move my ring finger up to the fourth string. I know it's only B flat minor, but Ernesto sounds like he's doing a melodic eulogy for Aldrich. The ghost of Aldrich and the koa wood have melded together. I can sense this ukulele changing history already. Harpo Giddyup will disrobe women around the globe with this tiny guitar and happiness will spread like an infection.

Aldrich would never have made a more important contribution to humanity. I've done a good deed.

I'll place my pinkie back onto the first string third fret and open up all the other strings. The infamous C major. In this context, playing the role of the major fifth to the minor tonic, it's as exotic as the island producing it. There Ernesto, you've played your first three chord melody in a minor key. Harpo has the masculine skills to take you into an ecstasy my poor dead fingers can't hope to achieve.

I'll play a little Hawaiian chunk stroke. It gives a dandy rhythm to a sad collection of chords. Aldrich, you're making us dance. Sometimes people dance because they're happy, sometimes because they're sad, and sometimes because they're too drunk to know the difference.

Aldrich, you will make the world dance every time they massage Ernesto.

You probably think I'm crazed. I shouldn't be talking to this little instrument like it's alive. Or if you're a musician, you probably understand. These instruments become windows into our souls and for those of you with souls, you're all the better for it. For the soulless, it's like talking to last week's lunch. And that's a happy memory.

Excuse me one more time. I need to box Ernesto up before the UPS man arrives.

Okay, I'm back. Sorry.

Ernesto is on his way to Chicagoland. The UPS driver looked particularly appetizing today. His legs are so tan and his body is so lean. I may have to find a way to get a piece of that guy some day. He always looks particularly yummy during the holidays when I see him more and he looks so frazzled from all the extra work. Maybe I'll make him Christmas dinner this year.

Christmas in Hawaii. Mele Kalikimaka.

I'm more of a fan of Easter, actually. That whole coming back from the dead story really gets me gushing. I'm looking forward to the apocalypse when we all come back from the dead to get our heavenly bodies. That should be quite a line-up. It'll make for a great story.

I've told my personal story to a few others before you. The story *Antonietta* by John Hersey is loosely based on my work in varnishing techniques. They created the movie the *Red Violin* based on his book. I guess Hersey thought violins made for better audiences than ukuleles. He probably felt more grey beards and English majors would open up their wallets for a violin story than a ukulele story. I'll bet he never saw Harpo Giddyup.

Marketing is one of my weak spots. When you spend most of your undead life pretending to be un-undead, it's best to keep away from all types of exposure. I'm better at being a hermetic craftsman than a flamboyant marketer.

The sun is setting and I can see the ocean from my workshop window. I'm not interested in the view of the water or the dazzling display of colors on the horizon. I'm mostly interested in the little girl rocking back and forth on the pink flying elephant on a spring over in the kiddy playground. She's making my mouth water. The apartment complex next door to my warehouse is the most affordable in the area and the most run down. So many families struggling to make it with so many kids. For a zombie, it's like a buffet.

I've got a soprano ukulele due for a client in Japan and I'm thinking that little girl would make the perfect finish. She could bring smiles and become a part of the Asian ukulele sensation. I think it would be good for her. I can almost taste her now. I can only imagine how good she'll sound.

Gladiator

Bobbi Dykema Katranis

Were we inmates, patients, or guests?
I remember faces, and names, but
seldom can I connect the two.
Were we lovers in a former life, or
just last week?
I remember a rose, perhaps another name,
and your lips, somewhere near the
base of my throat.
Was that your husband I met in the bar?
Are you for real? Are you somewhere
far away? Perhaps I
only dreamed it.
But the taste of your musk
is lingering in my mouth,
and I cannot escape these
eight new bruises on my belly,
hips, and thighs....

Do I still love you? Mirror image,
jealous friend? Will I take
your two hands between my
lips again? Will we be courtly
as two queens, facing off before
our dragons? Your kiss
embellishes my soul, so play it,
Sam. Repeat your ice cream
promises. Love me long time. Fill
me up with hope, or longing,
perfume, or desire.

Damned If You Do...

Amber Kemppainen

"You're being awfully quiet." Deep red fingernails tapped along with the music blaring from the car speakers.

Alan glanced at the busty redhead next to him before turning the music down again. "I've got a lot on my mind."

"Mmm baby, let me help you with that." She swung herself agilely into his lap, clearing the steering wheel with the ease of long practice. Her fingers began to massage his aching temples, while her hips slid seductively over his lap. Alan's head fell back as she began to work her magic. Taking advantage, she trailed kisses along his jaw and found the spot on his neck that always drove him crazy. Her teeth nipped gently; Alan caught his breath and pushed her up, kissing her regretfully.

"We need to talk."

Lori laughed. "Oh come on. It's a beautiful night. The moon is bright, the stars are out, we can see for miles from up here, and," her voice lowered to a husky whisper, "you have me all to yourself. What could possibly be that important?"

"I'm serious, Lori."

She sighed dramatically at his solemn tone and climbed back into the passenger seat. "Well?"

"You know how I feel about you, but now I need time to figure things out..."

She laughed again. "Why so serious? You're not breaking up with me," she stated confidently, tossing her hair over her shoulder.

"No, of course not!" he insisted, pulling her into an awkward hug around the gear shift. "It's just that with everything that's happened lately with...well, you know...my parents...the legal issues..."

She waved that aside casually. "Leave that stuff to the lawyers, they'll sort it out."

"Well there's Callie."

Immediately she tensed in his arms, her voice growing hard. "Your parents had no right to saddle you with her. You're only 18. Forcing you to..."

"I wanted to do this," he interrupted quietly, stroking her hair.

"What?" Her eyes narrowed with fury as she glared at him. "Why would you trade your freedom like that? What are you, some kind of idiot?"

His voice was quiet, willing her to understand. "She's my sister. No way I'd let her go into foster care when I'm perfectly capable of watching over her. She's not even in her teens. So I agreed to be her guardian just in case something happened to our parents."

"When exactly did you decide this?" She spat the words through clenched teeth. "And why didn't you tell me?"

"It wasn't your decision to make."

"You should have asked me how I felt about this."

"Lori..."

"We're dating!"

"Lori, calm down." He grabbed her arms and made her face him, his voice sharp. "I *don't* need this from you. I'm sorry, but right now I need to focus on helping Callie through this."

"So you're just ending this... ending us?" Her eyes bored into him, daring him to say the words.

He ran a hand through his long blond hair in frustration, turning away from her gaze. "I'm not ending anything. I'm just trying to do what needs to be done."

"I know what you need to do right now." She slid into his lap again. "I can give you everything you need. I'll take you away from all this agonizing and thinking." Her breath was warm against his ear as she rubbed along him like a cat. "Promise."

"Lori."

"Hmm?" She ran her tongue down the side of his neck, her teeth scraping the skin.

"Seriously. Stop."

"You...you're..." she was plainly shocked as he pushed her away. The shock quickly gave way to anger, sparks flashing in the depths of her eyes. "You're choosing that little brat over me?" She raised an eyebrow, her voice dripping with innuendo. "Why Alan, I didn't know you were that way..."

"Don't be sick!" Alan pushed her again, but she clung to him, fingernails digging into his back. Her teeth once again found his neck; this time she wasn't gentle. He flung her into the passenger seat and put a hand to a warm trickle of liquid beneath his ear. "Get out!"

Slowly Lori exited the car, her low, knowing laugh sending a shiver down his spine. She leaned back through the passenger window. "It's over when I say it's over," she stated, "and I say you're mine.

Forever." Her pink tongue darted out delicately as she licked blood off her lips.

Alan swore and threw the car into reverse, spewing gravel as he sped away. He couldn't shake the sound of her laughter achoing endlessly in his head. He drove quickly through the tight turns along the cliff down from the overlook. His neck stung and throbbed. He pressed his hand over the wound and swore again; it was still bleeding. He looked back over his shoulder, half-expecting to see her eyes staring after him.

Headlights coming around the curve ahead blinded him and he jerked the wheel to avoid the oncoming car. To his horror, the car went into a slide toward the guardrail. His mind raced with options he didn't have as the brakes refused to respond and the edge came closer and closer. The next few seconds stretched into eternity. Tires squealed. The passenger side crumpled inward with the shriek of twisting metal as the car broke through the flimsy barrier. His stomach lurched as the car spun, and broken glass filled the air as he was flung through the car window.

He tucked into a ball, but branches ripped at him, prying him open like a clam before he smashed to the ground. The night grew silent except for Lori's laughter still ringing in his ears. He fought to rise above the pain, but all he could do was lie there trying to breathe. When gravel crunched near his head, he managed to turn turned toward the sound. Lori came slowly into focus, a smile on her painted lips. "You and me? This is forever. I couldn't let you throw it away."

He opened his mouth to protest, but could only cough, pain tearing through him. "It's OK, baby," Lori cooed, absently removing a piece of glass from his head. Together they watched as blood dripped from it to the ground. "Just let it all go." She ran a hand through his hair, ignoring Alan's attempts to move away. She whispered in his ear, "I know you, Alan. You'll never be happy taking care of her. I know what you want, what you need. Don't worry, you'll have eternity to thank me."

"Poor Callie." Lori murmured, a malicious smile on her face. "What will she do now?"

Another bout of coughing brought white lights dancing in front of his eyes as he struggled to breathe. He couldn't die; Callie would be devastated. They'd just buried their parents, and he couldn't do this to her. He forced his eyes to focus on their surroundings. He knew this area; he just had to think. There. That rock formation. The highway made a series of switchbacks along the face of the cliff; he wasn't too far from one of them. Mustering his resolve, he painfully pulled his knees under him and met her gaze.

Lori frowned. "What are you doing?"

Alan ignored her as he lurched to his feet. He managed to stumble three steps toward the road before the agony drove him to his knees. He closed his eyes briefly, allowing himself a momentary respite from the pain.

Lori stood over him, fuming. "You don't get it, do you? You're dead! You were in a car crash and you died. This is your way out! You don't have to baby-sit that sister of yours anymore. You're free!" She scowled as he forced himself to his feet again. "Look, if you're going to be difficult about this, I can take care of Callie."

"Stay away from her," Alan managed to choke out.

"You need to give her up," she insisted, pushing him back down with her foot. "I don't share what's mine."

"I'm not..." His chest seized. Once, twice, and stopped. Everything stopped. He couldn't move. His eyes were open, watching the rain coming down. The impact of the raindrops was like pellets on his skin, but he couldn't blink, he was frozen in place.

"You *are* mine, and now it's forever." She patted him on the shoulder. "Don't fight this, baby. I'll pick you up in a few days."

Lori left, tossing a careless wave over her shoulder as she went. If this was death, there was no tunnel, no white light. He could see everything, hear everything, but could do nothing but watch as the world went on without him. Bustling paramedics gave up on him, policemen came to make a report, and he saw it all until someone closed his eyes. Then he felt movement; they were taking him somewhere. He thought he would go crazy as he fought to see, to move, to tell someone that he was still alive! Didn't they know? Couldn't they tell?

Finally, exhausted from his efforts, he let his awareness drift inwards: his body was trying to heal. Something was moving through his veins with the efficiency and knowledge of a master surgeon. Repairing this, closing that, but it felt like something far away. A distrubing pattern began to emerge. As the pain from his injuries subsided, another pain was starting to grow. Inside, his guts were twisting, crying out for something. Though the pain grew, Alan felt sleep overtake him.

He awoke to thunder ringing in his ears. The thunder settled into a steady beckoning rhythm, his body trembling as it called to him. Thump, thump pause. Thump, thump pause. He could feel something coursing through him, bidding him to act. His fingers clenched tight in response and he savored the movement. His eyes were still closed; his eyelids impossibly heavy. A muffled noise close to his ear drowned out the thunder. Warm liquid fell on his face and he forced his mind to work. He heard footsteps and every muscle in his body clenched at the smell of Lori's perfume.

"Lori, I really appreciate your offer to help with all the arrangements, but I really need some time alone with Alan." Callie's voice was tight and shaky as another tear fell on his face. "I just can't believe he's gone."

"I know. I'm so sorry. I called 911 as soon as he left, but I didn't think he'd really go through with it."

Abruptly the drops stopped falling. "What are you talking about?"

"He said he didn't want the burden. I guess he thought this was the only way..." Lori's voice trailed off.

She was enjoying this, he could tell by the barely concealed smirk in her voice. He could almost hear his sister's heart breaking in response.

"The police said it was an accident. The brakes failed. Alan would *never* do this on purpose." Callie's voice was quiet, but firm.

"Oh honey. I'm sorry. I didn't mean to upset you." Lori said. "I'm sure he didn't mean it that way."

"He promised me."

Alan's fists tightened in response to the pain in Callie's voice. He wanted to kill Lori for putting it there though he'd never considered hurting a woman before.

"Promises are meant to be broken." The air in the room altered, thickening with coiled excitement. Alan felt the change in Lori: the urge to hunt, to kill. He recognized it in himself; his new instincts pushing him to act. Panic filled him and he forced his eyes open, his body up and out of the coffin. His gaze shifted between the two girls.

"Alan? Oh my God!" Callie launched herself at him, rocking him backward: her tears now of joy. "You're alive! I prayed and prayed..." She hugged him tight as if afraid he wasn't real.

"It's OK. I'm alive." He returned the hug automatically, her scent washing over him as pain lanced through his jaw.

Over Callie's head, he saw Lori tap her teeth with a long, polished nail, her grin wicked. Alan stiffened as his tongue ran across his own sharpened canines. Callie reacted immediately. "You're still hurt. God! What am I thinking? I'll call an ambulance." She reached into her purse and yanked out her cell phone. Lori took it from her and pocketed it.

"Sorry sweetie. I'd hoped to take care of this before he woke up, but this might be better." She inclined her head toward Callie. "You know what to do, baby; it's in your blood."

"Alan?"

Lori chuckled at Callie's confusion. "He's mine now, sweet-cheeks—a vampire. And you, well, you're just lunch."

Alan stared down into his sister's green eyes and realized with a shock that he was reading her mind. She was concerned, but it wasn't for herself, it was for him. She trusted him. Looking away, his gaze met Lori's and defiantly, he shoved Callie behind him.

Lori's smile faded, her eyes flashing with anger. "What are you thinking? You need this. Do it!"

"No."

"Don't say no to me! I made you! You don't *get* to say no to me!" Lori's face reddened as she shrieked. Alan braced himself as she launched herself at him, her nails growing into talons. Small hands thrust him aside, and he gaped at Callie as she planted the wooden crucifix from his coffin in Lori's chest. Lori gasped, clinging to the girl's's hair to hold herself upright. "You're both fools! He'll turn on you the moment the cravings get too bad. You'll see." Her voice was a malicious thread of sound. Alan dragged Callie free, watching in horror as lori crumbled into ash.

"Cal..." he began as she pulled away from him, her eyes shining with unshed tears. Unwittingly, his eyes focused on the white-knuckled grip his sister still had on the crucifix. "She's wrong about me," Alan said her with a forced smile, willing it to be so.

"Is she?" Reaching out, she touched one of his teeth and shivered as it lengthened in response. "I don't know what to believe." Her gaze strayed to the ash at her feet.

"You can trust me."

She stared at the floor for a long moment before meeting his eyes squarely. "Promise me. Swear you'll never hurt anyone."

"I don't..."

"Promise me," Callie pleaded. Fresh tears streamed down her face as she searched his face for reassurance.

Though his body growled with hunger, Alan pulled his sister to him and held her tight as her body shook with sobs. The crucifix she held between them felt burning hot, and he whispered the only thing he could say.

"I promise."

Legitimate Objects of Desire

Helga Kidder

*Forbidden fruit a flavor has
that lawful orchards mocks;
how luscious lies the pea within
the pod that duty locks!*
−EmilyDickinson

Passing the produce, pomegranates trigger
urgency of desire. And above, a sign

Do Not Handle. Right & left other women
choose peaches, count dark purple plums

into plastic bags, place them carefully in carts.
Mine is still empty. Rhubarb blushes

in front of me as I watch a man extend his
right hand deep into lemon-laced broccoli.

How easy the poor choice is. Should I tell him
rule number one, *Never Shop Hungry*?

Around me others collect their next meal while
I pretend interest in skin-thin sliced cold cuts

at the delicatessen. Should I also bag lemony
florets or give in to overpriced pomegranate?

Pulpy thickness & seeds between two people,
wild sweetness spilling everywhere.

Why do we insist walking back to the first time?
Find recourse in staples & live by the rule book,

was Mother's advice. My cart is still empty.
Legitimate or not, objects of desire blemish

from too much touch or spoil inside out,
given time. Either way, we pay the price.

Tree Naked in Winter

Robert Lawrence

Layer upon layer of
grey-brown branches wave
against blue-white sky;
pattern within pattern
intricate
like congealed lightning.
High up, the thin strands
of an abondoned bird's nest
flutter
in the stiff wind.

Standing here,
even in my down coat,
I feel chilled.
Imagine one so entranced
by a tree naked in winter
that he fails to go indoors.
When I reach home,
I will drink hot tea,
sit by the fireside,
and meditate
on how often beauty
is interlaced with danger.

The Magic Edge
Harmon Leete*

There is a magic in the edge of things.
When seen against a surface far below
it calls your eyes to come, look down, way down,
and, when they are transfixed, tugs at your body to move closer,
to lean over and surrender to the air.
It fills the moment on a mountaintop
before the giddy drop to   the first bite of skis,
and on the top of crumbling, steep-staired temples at Uxmal and
Angkor Wat ,
while going up is easy, when you turn, you quickly back
against the wall, away from small, hand-waving figures far below.
Roller coasters bring a different kind of fascinating terror,
for falling is inevitable once you've gotten on, but everyone survives.
Airlines and tall buildings are another backward step,
imposing sturdy barriers between
your fragile body and free fall. For that,
you fasten straps around your chest or ankles
and with a canopy or long elastic cords
take leave of all your senses and step off.
But these flights pale beside the freedom
waiting in the boundless corridors of sleep
where easily your widespread arms can touch the filmy stuff of clouds
and, banking, let you survey towns and countrysides below
in blissful, soaring moments that grow labored
as first gentle and then stronger arm-beats are required
to stay aloft, then desperate, violent flailing as the sky gives way
and all the magic ends....

Never Another Wild Rose...

Ellaraine Lockie

picked on the Montana prairie
That I won't see blood
dripping down milkweed white legs

The woman's eyes closed
to the open invasion
Thorned weapon scoring her thighs

like a flank roast
he wants medium rare
Its sap sucked up for an appetizer

My Band-Aid stretching
over the bite of a resistant rose
Sealing the ache inside

An Apple's First Fall

Jacqueline M. Lyon

Spinning by its stem,
the Red Delicious twirls.
The dancing fruit is tempted
by fingers of a school girl.

He spies the crimson ball
set on an ink-stained stage,
prancing directed by a doll
of a most precarious age.

Twisted by intent,
the sturdy stem snaps.
The daring fruit is sent
into the uniformed lap.

His fingers grip the stiff, white chalk,
and turning to the board, they write
the simple words of *Paradise Lost*,
the blind man's poem of a hellish fight.

He hears hungry whispers from the Snake—
A virgin core holds the fertile seed,
her tender flesh is yours to take,
Now follow Lucifer's lead.

Held by the pressed plaid pleats
rests the florid fruit.
She shines the smooth, red meat
with her parochial juice.

Echoing from the slate gray board,
the Serpent sounds his call.
Will He taste the sweet rewards
of the apple's foul first Fall?

Daughter of the Sea

Reflections on *The Little Mermaid* by Hans Christian Andersen
Jessica L. Maynard

It is the difference between my life and your death.
This knife, forged of slate and conch shell,
is an intriguing thing, as delicate as it is poisonous.
If I hold the handle to my ear,
I can hear the splitting of my sisters' hair,
the crooning cackle of the Sea Witch,
the sigh from your new bride's chest.

It is the difference between your life and mine.
These legs, which you take for granted
are like broken shards of glass to me.
You danced, and I did, too. That night
when all we could think of was the sea,
the *sea* with no mention of princesses, or temple girls.
This knife is the difference between you and I.
So delicate, it was crafted from the sea, (as was I)
and will not commit such monstrosities.
That is the way of my father.
This blade of the sea, so close to your cheek,
 will not take you in this wave of sorrow.
It is not my way.

It is the difference between your life and my death,
This foolish love.

Uncommon Bond

Kathleen McElligott

The old house is quiet,
the bedroom dark
as I drift into the chasm
of sleep.

Passing through the gauzy plane,
suspended;
no expectations.
No sorrow.

A child, crouched in the corner
arranges toy soldiers;
warring armies,
preparing for battle.

An aura surrounds him
as he works at play;
his old, worn cap
on pale gold tufts.

Slowly he looks up,
eyes fever-bright.
With outstretched hand
he offers a soldier.

I reach for his pudgy fingers,
my heart expands with longing.
Slowly, his image fades—
the cruel night returns.

How Do You Cook an Artichoke?

Ann McGovern

It's bubbling now, in the sauce pan,
probably too small a pot.
Do I cover it or not.

I prefer it in the restaurant,
all the tough leaves off. On bone china,
in flattering light, it looks exotic.

I wonder about the statistics.
How many artichoke deaths,
planned or accidental.

At home, I'm afraid of it.
I could pierce my throat from its sharp purple edges
or choke on its pale yellow fuzz.

Maybe I'd better call the elevator man.
Living alone is scary.
Planned or accidental.

Job Hunting

Ann McGovern

"If you want a safe job, sell shoes."
But danger lies between painted toes.
Catastrophe circles her slim ankles.
She lifts one leg, showing thigh and higher.

"If you want a safe job, be a doorman."
But then you wear hot uniforms in summer
freeze in winter when you open doors,
smile at the tenant who tried to get you fired.

"If you want a safe job, fillet fish."
But dull knives cause major mishaps.
You'll smell fishy for days
not to mention mercury and low pay.

"If you want a safe job, clean the graveyard."
But listen. The dead are talking to you.
And dark descends quickly.
Your turn.

Witnesses in Wisconsin

Lylanne Musselman

We witnessed the sun's last gasp in Wisconsin,
smothered by scruffy clouds headed south
in a hurry, as we traveled north
bound to friends in Fort Atkinson.

Sirens warned us, surrounded
by Mother Nature's twisted escapees,
armed and dangerous—who tip cows,
ransack houses and toss cars for thrills.

We were hostage, blinded by rain
and cursed with hail, easy targets
for apple shrapnel and fallen tree bazookas.

Too late to change our course. No turning back. We had to reach Sandy and Brian's,
safe on Rock River's bank,
where laughter rolls,
good food flows as cats grow to our laps,
and on clear nights we watch
fireflies burn the moon,
flickering glitter upon the water.

Dear Stranger

Diana M. Raab

Your eyes spoke
a language I understood,

the only rope stretching
between us, everything else

separated by a universe
and droves of years.

Your tall, dark and handsome
youth wanted me in a big way

and a bigger way when I sat alone
as my husband meandered into the w.c.
and you gave me a moment of you.

I pushed to ignore the short-lived
intensity of our magnetic attraction

because in the end it wouldn't matter,
but as a woman entering her sixth decade

your desire ripped me from my complacency,
until there in The Naples airport you put on your

sunglasses and wheeled your suitcase out
from baggage claim, turned around

and slid them to the tip of your nose,
licked your lips from side to side,

smiled and walked outside, thrusting into your
world and sending me back into mine.

The Subjectivity of Love and Art

Jessica Bane Robert

From ice encased firewood in nor'easterly wind
my father stormed, his eyebrow an easel point.
My heart stiffened like silverware in the slammed drawer,
trembled like the broken dish on its open shelf,
stopped like the clock on the marble-top table.
He raged past like a tempest to the studio.

A bottle of brandy by his stool, a stick to steady
his cracked and bleeding hand, the afternoon
of pouring and painting began. I hid above
(and beside him, my portrait by his shoulder—
four years old—a sweet, crooked smirk,
beret cocked to one side). His brushes dripped;

I cried. Too cold outside, I crouched in the eaves
amidst the dusty stacks—nudes, unicorns, and
dead uncles all in decay. Cemeteries toppled,
mantis skeletons, and Lucifer smoldering
in the city square, eyes burning like cigarettes.
I dreamed of summer's green shade...When the fog

of turpentine and drink shrouded every pore,
our paths crossed in the studio door. He held me
in the dizzying smell, the electric flicker,
and he cried. Molding my form on his knee,
rough hands framing my cheeks, he asked: *Do you know
how much I love you?* I answered with a kiss

tasting the salty pigments of our abstract fears.

⋮

114

⋮

Sheol

Kimberly Raven

This story is about a quest, the journey into a world of gnarled tree
stumps and two suns that don't light the land beyond shadow.
This place is damned by the gods, if the gods have taken enough time
to grant it such, and I have journeyed a thousand miles in search of
her: a woman who can help me, or so I've heard. She is called Hebre,
and she is esteemed to be a 115 years old, a conniving and unpredictable
old coot who would cut off your ear if it suited her, and now, before
me, between valleys and massive rises of earth—I have found her.

The town where she lives—a place called Sheol—lies a few
thousand feet below the ledge where I stand, a town buried within a
deep crevice that falls sharply, and it clings to the cliff face as would a
desperate child to an unwilling mother.

I pause, wishing I could take that one step...embrace those
thousand feet as my own, but even suicide would not be enough.

Forgive me. I get morbid at times. I allow myself such from time
to time but do my best not to make it a habit. They call me the
Intruder—and in this dark world I am just that: an intruder. This land
isn't mine, certainly, and I would never wish to claim it as such; but
memories of my own world have grown distant. I hardly remember
who I am, who I was. How did it happen? What awful thing did I do
to get here? I pray to the northern sun, asking for return to my own
world, but she doesn't answer. I am not a religious man. Perhaps she
knows this. She mocks me, even fears me. Or perhaps I don't come
from any world, and she is too kind to shed tears for me.

My prayer doesn't take long. When I am finished I rise to my
feet and take the path down to Sheol. In this land there are no cars or
helicopters. Only paths. Weak, insubstantial paths that quickly lead
you astray if you let them. It takes hours to descend, between dead-
ends and half-humored falls, and my arrival reveals the same old
tragedy: a carcass lies at the bottom of the path—a goat, bled dry by
the thirst of wolves, its eyes fixed in a glassy stare.

Sheol is silent. Its inhabitants know of my coming. They have
boarded up their windows and doors, doing their best to protect

themselves, but I need their kindness—I am hungry—and once again I am left begging for food. On occasion someone slides a piece of bread under the door—as though it were an offering to the gods, to me, something meant to appease and keep me away—and I eat the food in silence. No. I am not evil. But I don't blame them for thinking me so.

Today there is an open door.

"So you are the *Intruder*," comes a voice. It is not a question. "You look human. I hadn't expected that."

I am human, I think. I don't say it out loud.

The old woman invites me into her house. I lower my eyes, as always, but I can see her hands, ten trembling and thin, bony fingers wrapped about the handle of a kitchen knife. I can imagine Hebre's eyes, alert and intelligent, devious things buried in a devious face. I have not looked at a face for many years—not without it happening—but even then I dream of them, obsess about them, even try to imagine what a face is like by the sound of a voice, the way someone moves, or the scent of his body left behind after he runs away from me.

"It just takes an exchange of glances, doesn't it?" she says. I don't answer. She knows already. The old lady is silent a moment, standing before me with a bent shadow that speaks of severe osteoporosis and a cane that somehow holds her up. "How dare you come looking for me," she says finally.

"I had no choice."

"And what do you want?"

"I need a way out," I say.

Hebre almost chuckles. "You won't find a way out with me...at least not a fair one. It is your fault that our skies are dark, that the land is barren. It is your fault we are dying. Do you think you deserve such? A way out? Ha! You aren't worthy of a way out."

"Please." I am begging, like I always do. I study the floor, the sink, the fire burning in the corner. An emaciated chicken has been plucked and is roasting itself into a small meal. A dying plant sits on the table. There is a sheet hanging across the back of the room. Through the holes I can see a bed behind it. I look at everything except her. I will not catch her gaze. I will not do this. "I need your help."

"My help? That I conjure up some magic to forgive you?" She is watching me. I sigh, keeping my eyes low. "So it is magic you want," she continues. "That isn't too difficult. Though it won't be altogether pleasant, and certainly not forgiving."

"Then get it done, old woman."

She doesn't answer. Instead she sits down, coughing, resting uncomfortably on a weakened stool, and she whispers something under her breath, singing with a soft, rough voice, singing a song of songs, and it fills the small hut with a coldness that hadn't been there before. It isn't kind. I know that. But a gift is a gift, and I am prepared to accept anything.

The song ends, but she doesn't say anything for a few minutes. The air is still cold, and the silence hangs powerfully in the air. "You want help?" she says softly. "Fine. The God of Disease will rise up and help you himself. Now he comes, without pity, and he won't have problems finding you. Your pathetic soul will guide him."

I'm not sure why I do it. Perhaps it is a reflex, that natural pull to the eyes of a voice that pains you. Or maybe I am angry. I want to see the person, the owner of the voice that is hurting me, find her eyes, see her crooked teeth and the foul-smelling hood she has over her head. I want to see the trembling lips. I want to see a face. I want to see a human being that doesn't die the moment I lay eyes upon her.

I catch her gaze, and Hebre's face twists into a grin—of course she is expecting it. And, as always, it happens. This curse, this affliction. I watch her, stepping back as far as the over-pressured hut will let me, perhaps trying to escape but not letting myself do so, and Hebre's eyes cloud over with tears. Not forgiving tears. These tears are the type that sting when they touch you, that reek of hate and vengeance, and once again—as I have done thousands of times before—I let it happen.

There is the sudden smell of loosened bowels and urine. I help her to the bed, but she claws at me with such fury that the scratches draw blood. "You will rot away into nothing," she whispers, then screams loudly as it takes over: Hebre's skin turns red, prickly, then rises into blisters, face, arms, chest blistering over, blister upon blister, and yes, as always, the blisters open, weeping thick fluid and leaving raw flesh underneath, scathing the healthy skin to the side, and the old lady cries loudly, too loudly. I leave the wretched woman's side before I see the rest.

In the past I've tried to save them. Tried to get them through the vomiting and diarrhea, the infection, gangrene, and amputations...through the screaming and agony...but they don't survive. They suffer, and they never survive.

I am trembling as I leave. I walk slowly, and soon I hear it: a hoarse, raspy breath upon breath, and in the distance I can see it in the shadows, with hands gnarled into crooked stumps. The air is filled with the scent of decay. The creature is massive, and it is following me.

I almost laugh as I wait for Hebre's gift to find me.

Voices in the Fire

Lynn Veach Sadler

Come by the fire. Never step into the shadows.
Warm yourself in grace. Hear my tale,
your grandmother's warning.

Do you hear wind? Fire's crackle?
Be not alarmed by the Old Crone's cackle.
My mother bested her, passing protection
from me to mine and you. If the Old Crone
loudens, stick your fingers in your ears.
That gentle tap, tap, tapping?
That's your grandmother. I own this hearth.

The night they pitched their battle,
I was a little tyke like you.
The Old Crone had lost her child,
prayed to Beelzebub to purchase me.
My mother and the Old Crone went
at each other like two cats in a circle.
Skin and sinew, blood and bones,
they wore each other down to voices.

Oh, sweet child, don't cringe!
Your grandmother will protect you.
When you hear the spit and crackle,
when the embers come at you,
the Old Crone's there with her minions.
But when the fire is all-of-a-piece
toasting you, your grandmother's home
keeping Old Crone and her Beelzebub
outside the firelight in darkness eternal!
But pray, be careful. Be warned!

The Dustoff

George Samerjan

The village seamstress crafted a holster for a submachine gun,
she stuffed piasters back in my pocket, smiled,
our jeep lurched from Vo Xu's market,
shrieks of wailing women braked us,
they showed us the house,
dust hung in the air,
a man tightened by pain knelt in the blood of his wife's bed sheets,
Dustoff!
Carrying her to our Jeep, placing her across the altar of our radios,
calling our prayers for her aloft,
running alongside the Jeep like benign centaurs to the landing zone,
a whirlwind of dust and pebbles scratching our bodies,
her blood caking upon our hands we carried her stretcher,
the hovering craft gently lifted,
soon she became a dot traversing the clouds,
we drove back to the outpost,
silently listened to the hiss of meat grilling,
drank beer in the twilight,
and felt the beads of water slide through our clenched fingers like tears.

Spider in My Tub

Art Schwartz

Small worrier
shrunk to a point
abruptly plunging in
a sudden marvelous display

Or demonstration
against trespasses
within your house and
living space, o small experiencer,

It's this dazzling downward swoop,
and not the skill of your many legs,
nor your silky, sticky craftsmanship,
nor the cunning capture of hapless flies.

It's this soundless
howl from a fellow possessor
of partial knowledge concerning the danger
inside my tub, with which I sympathize.

Fields Where Glory Does Not Stay
Lones Seiber

I've been racing all my life; it's in my blood; from go carts when I was a kid to the All-Pro Series, which is a stepping stone to the big time, it's been my life, and although my wife Brenda hasn't said as much, this will probably be my last race. I know she's tired of living in the rented doublewide down by the river. With the money coming in, we could have a house of our own, not just struggling to make ends meet, if it wasn't for the racing. She's been patient, more than most women would have, waiting for us to turn the corner like I promised, but it just hasn't happened.

And then my brother Larry, who's also my mechanic, told me I'd have to finish fifth or better in today's race, otherwise Jimmy's going to pull his sponsorship. That was right after I'd qualified seventh. The Jimmy he was speaking of is Jimmy Stubblefield of Stubblefield's Muffler Shop down in Due West. So if we lose him, that'll be that.

Today's race is just one of several in the All-Pro Series, but it's at the Easley-Pickens Speedway, which is only ten miles from where we live, so it's sort of a home stand. The All-Pro is a series for young drivers on the way up, some with factory backing, like Jason Taylor and Danny Pressley, both of whom will probably move up to Grand National within the next year or two, and for those on the way down, like Jody Ripley, the headliner for the race, giving him a chance to keep doing the only thing he knows and maybe a little hope. Back in '81 he ran a few races in Winston Cup, but since then, it's been a slow slide back to Easley-Pickens. They say he's divorced and got married grandkids.

Easley-Pickens isn't what it used to be, wasn't always small potatoes. A lot of the legends started here, their names on the wall around the track: Neil Bonnett, David Pearson, Harry Gant, Morgan Shepherd. There's also one that most people outside Easley-Pickens wouldn't recognize: Billy Joe Moffett. He won last year. I was here. Finished twelfth after starting twentieth, my best showing in three years of All-Pro. I was happy; Brenda said she was proud of me and gave me a kiss, but I know she was disappointed in the check, all the things it wouldn't buy: a dishwasher, a clothes dryer, a set of new Firestones for the Taurus instead of recaps, and so on.

Nobody had ever heard of Moffett. He was from somewhere up the Saluda Grade, just over the North Carolina line, apple country. Flat Rock, I think. That sounds right, anyway. I remember the sponsor even: Stella's Nail Salon. Looked like they'd painted it on the doors and hood freehand. We all got a kick out of that. It wasn't in the same class as Quality Care or Hooters, or even Stubblefield's Muffler Shop, but I understood: you take what you can get. His car wasn't much: not trimmed out, dented. I'm surprised they even let him qualify. In the old days they wouldn't have, but things being the way they are, they had to fill out the field. It was his first big race I learned later. They said he'd run in Asheville and at dirt tracks here and there.

He qualified somewhere in the back, behind me anyway. People never knew what happened, how he got on the lead lap even, but that's what the charts said. Maybe he only changed two tires toward the end or gambled on fuel, or maybe he was just that damned good, but there he was, on the final lap, in fourth place behind Pressley. I was a lap down and behind him when he slipped below Pressley going into turn three, his left-side tires dipping below the white line. That's illegal if you gain position, but what can I say? It's Easley-Pickens. I went with him to maybe pick up a spot. In turn four he caught a flyer and pulled away from me and slid high, but then he cut low again behind Ripley and Taylor who were side by side heading for the checkered. I figured that was it: no way he could get by those two; besides, third place for some country boy in his first race? Anybody would have been happy with that; I would have been happy with that, more than happy, but then he dove low again, the back end squirrelly, on the edge so to speak, passing on the underside of Taylor, coming off his rear like a slingshot, catching them both by a foot or so at the flag.

And then the place went nuts. Beer cans came flying over the fence. People dancing in the stands. It was like a fucking fairy tale, except it wasn't: Everybody was surprised he won, and Taylor must have been surprised, too, keeping his attention on Ripley, never imagining anyone would have balls enough to challenge them, especially on the low side, because at the checkered, he eased up and drifted down, catching the right rear quarter-panel of Moffett's car as it slipped past underneath.

"I never saw him," Taylor said afterwards, and his eyes said he hadn't.

Everybody concluded later that it had been a racing incident. Nobody was to blame.

It wasn't much of a crash as crashes go, nothing like Davey Allison's end over end wreck at Pocono after Darryl Waltrip clipped his rear fender; how many times did he flip? Nineteen, twenty, more? People still disagree, but they all remember his thumbs up as the stretcher wheeled him away. Nothing like Rusty Wallace at Talladega, hanging on as he went airborne, the car destroying itself as it tumbled almost the length of a straightaway, him walking away with a smile and not a scratch. No. Moffett slid easily up the track and skidded nose-first along the wall, the front end crumpling back to the engine, but not all at once. Absorbing the impact, as it was supposed to. Not what you'd call a violent crash. Something you'd see at least once in any race and not think a thing about. I'd seen worse. A lot worse. I remember feeling envious. A win in his first try. I'd been sweating my ass off going on three years, and for what? Twelfth! I pulled into the pits after the cool-down lap. Larry tried to sound upbeat, saying something about how it could have been worse, not how it could have been better. And then we all stood around talking, the drivers, the pit crews, mostly about what might have been, before loading up and heading home.

"Where the hell did he come from?" Taylor said, rubbing his hair with a towel as he swigged a Mountain Dew. No one seemed to know. "A hell of a drive."

"Phenomenal!" is what the fat broadcaster with no hair from Motor Sports Network said as he talked to other drivers. "Who the hell is he?" He was trying to fill time, making it as big a deal as he could to keep folks from changing the station while waiting for Moffett to climb out of the car. Who was he? No one knew. I tried to remember him, what he looked like. Counting off the faces I knew in my mind. I must have seen him, around the pits, in the drivers' meeting maybe, but then he was a nobody. No reason to remember.

I might've been one of the first to suspect that something wasn't quite right when people gathered around the car longer than they should, the catch nets down, their heads stuck through the windows. I mean, he should have been out, jumping up and down on the hood, pumping his fists, smiling toward the sky, climbing the fence, maybe even crying. It happens, but then, when they stretched a sheet to block a view of the driver's window, everybody in the pits stopped talking and just stared toward turn one. My stomach felt as if I were dropping too fast in an elevator. The P.A. announcer, his voice cheerful, said Moffett had been injured, as if everything was going to be okay; they always say that so the fans can leave not blaming the track, but we knew better. As an ambulance took its time backing up the slope, the attendants in no hurry with the gurney when it stopped, a young woman with long, straight hair, wearing a loose, green dress and flip-flops, struggled up the embankment, falling to her hand a couple of times, before an older man in an orange vest held her close, pushing her away from the car as she beat her temples with her fists and screamed. Her purse fell, the contents scattering down the track. A boy behind her, around eight or so, wearing a yellow tee shirt, cutoff jeans, and no shoes, dropped to his knees and gathered everything back into her purse. Then he held it in one hand, her arm with the other.

———

The cars are positioned on the pit lane. I'm inside, just waiting. It's hotter than hell, but I don't mind. Seems like this is the only place where things still make sense.

"We're about to turn the corner. I can feel it," I keep telling Brenda, but it's a lot of bullshit, and she knows it. Brenda's no dumb ass.

She's not here today. It's the first race she's missed. She has Sundays off; she might go in before or afterwards, just to see that things are running smooth, but they have some new machines being installed on her floor at the hospital today, and she said she had to be there, her being in charge and all. She tried explaining about the new equipment, why it's so important, even drew me some pictures. Has something to do with premature babies, with giving them a better shot.

"And it's about time," she said and nodded and smiled over what she'd drawn, as if she was proud of herself.

"Yeah," I said, as if I understood, but I didn't. I never finished high school.

She's a supervisor at the hospital over in Anderson now. When we first got married, she was kind of an orderly, doing things nobody else would.

"I'm tired of going nowhere," she said after about a year and took some courses over at the junior college. She studied nights and weekends and made good grades, and that seems to have made the difference. That's when she caught fire. They promoted her pretty quickly after that. She's been employee of the month a bunch of times. Had her own parking spot out front with her name on the curb. She took me by to see it and take a snapshot the first time she won. Now she's in charge of the maternity ward. She hires and fires and sets the hours for everybody on the floor. Six months ago they sent her to school in Columbia for a week, something about personnel management. They paid for everything, even the phone calls back home at night.

I operate a backhoe for Shirl Whitson putting in septic tanks, but I don't work every day, just when he needs me. It's what I know.

She cooked me some pancakes and bacon for breakfast this morning. All she had was a slice of cantaloupe and a banana.

"Good luck today," she said as she picked up her pocketbook and keys.

"I'll need it," I said, but she was already out the door.

She was dressed up, like for church. With the weight she's lost, she had to buy some new clothes, the kind you'd wear for business.

She looked really nice. They even got her one of those computers you can fold up and carry around.

A couple of nights back, she said that the Hospital Director might be promoted to the headquarters in Charlotte to take charge of the whole operation, that if it happened, he would want her to go along as his executive assistant.

"It would be like a dream come true!" she said and grabbed me in a bear hug.

"What would I do in Charlotte?" I asked. She didn't answer; just smiled.

───────

We're told to get ready to start the engines and clear the pits. Larry sticks his head through the window just before I put the net up.

"Come in early, around lap 30," he yells, his eyes all watery, and pats my shoulder, "and go easy on the tires!"

I nod and give him a thumbs up, but I don't see that strategy's going to make any difference at this point. I'll see Elvis before I finish fifth or better in this fucking race.

Somebody raps the microphone and then clears his throat through the P.A.

"Gentlemen! Start your engines!" he announces, trying to sound real serious, like something important is fixing to be decided.

The official standing at the end of pit road signals us out with a furled flag in each hand to start the formation lap. The sound of all those engines revving causes my heart to race and makes me forget everything else for just a moment.

Most drivers have some sort of good luck charm with them or a ritual they go through while they're sitting in the car waiting for the signal to roll off. Some pray; others keep a lucky coin in their pocket or have a picture stuck in some crack just above the windshield. I never found nothing that worked, so I don't bother. I've heard that Jody Ripley counts backwards from a hundred by sevens before each race and then smiles when he gets to two, as if he's convinced it's never going to end. Maybe we won't admit it out loud, but the rest of us know it's just a matter of time before we have to call it a day. Dale Earnhardt on turn three at Daytona? Fireball Roberts on lap seven at Charlotte? Even Billy Joe Moffett last year here at Easley-Pickens? They're the lucky ones.

I am Ripped
Susan Baller-Shepard

I am cut. My abs grooved like the San Andreas fault,
my trapezius earth-strong, delts and quads chiseled taut.
I shove plates over with one hand,
what it takes others two to budge.
I am focus, drive. I powerlift.
My BMI is enviable. No anabolics.
Too little fat to ovulate, my body is rock,
with nothing sculpted but forged,
a vein of iron runs through.
Men move, when they are on
the bench I want to use.

Our Similar Genomes
Susan Baller-Shepard

The ache—
in the chimpanzee hugging her dead baby until
the zoo keeper tranquilizes her, takes away those
threadbare shreds—
is one I know firsthand,
holding close those I've loved until all that is left
is faded and worn from hauling and mauling of
memory.
She knew—
that her baby would stay dead, it wasn't as if carrying
it
around would bring it back to life. She just wasn't
ready
to give up yet.

Witchy Wager

Excerpted from *Jezebels of the Earth*
Wade Sikorski

Reverend Frogge couldn't get the witch out of his mind. She haunted him in his dreams, while he was writing sermons, while he was reading the Bible, and, especially, while he was praying. He tried to banish her from his thoughts by focusing on his work, but invariably they drifted back to her, and her defiant public wager that she would have sex with him. Despite himself, he found himself thinking about the way her nipples poked through her halter-top, the shape of her hips, the contours of her smile, and the warmth and smell of her body when she was near. Maybe she hadn't cast any actual spells on him, as she claimed, but she didn't need to. Her body, even fully clothed, was spell enough, her manner worse. The witch just presumed she owned his thoughts. She knew what effect she had on him, and she didn't let him pretend otherwise.

Under the spell of her body, he could only pretend to listen to people when he was counseling them in his office, and too often, he would find himself awkwardly silent while they expected his comments. As they waited, the silence would drag on, giving lie to his pretense, until they did something to catch his attention. Most people were polite, even though they suspected, but the widow Foster got rude one day. She snapped her fingers at him. "Wake up you fool," she demanded, as only the elderly can. "You should be thinking about your wife, not that witch."

"I'm sorry," he said. "But I wasn't thinking about Anaya," realizing too late his answer amounted to a confession. "Honest," he said when Widow Foster gave him a don't-con-me look.

"You need to read your own sermons on adultery," she snorted. "You have a beautiful wife, a lovely daughter, and a reputation to keep. You'll lose them all if you let that Jezebel run your life—her and that obscene wager she made against your soul. She wants to destroy you, to drag your soul through the mud, down into Hell. You know she does, everyone does. Snap out of it! You're supposed to be an example for us all."

Reverend Frogge decided that denial was futile. "You're right, you're right." He nodded. "I have too much to lose."

"Not to mention your immortal soul. The Devil would love to have you in hell, humiliated."

"Please," he said, raising his hand to stop her, "I know, I know, really I do. I get it."

"No you don't!" she snapped. "The Devil has his claws out for you and you don't see it. He is waging a war against us, our whole church, all this witchcraft and whoring, and you are the primary target. If he takes you down, he can take us all down. You have to stop this wager." Her small, bony frame was taut with indignation. Her screeching reminded him of the wicked witch in The Wizard of Oz. "Everyone is talking about it," she continued, "for hundreds of miles around, betting when that Jezebel is going to get you into her bed. I wouldn't be surprised if Katie Couric, that liberal wench on CBS, did a story on it, and we became the laughing stock of the entire nation." Reverend Frogge blinked. The widow was becoming more and more irritating, pushing him to the edge. "Make the Jezebel stop this wager. Get a lawyer, sue her! Or better yet, have The Priesthood deal with her. They know what to do. She'll be in Hell before she can do any more harm."

"Stop right there," he said, finally having had enough. "That kind of talk won't be tolerated. I'll stop the bet, and I won't need The Priesthood to do it. Now go."

The Widow Foster slowly got up out of her seat, smugly satisfied she had finally hit pay dirt. "I'll pray for you," she said, pretending virtue.

"I'll pray for you, too," he said, as unconvincingly. As she turned her back, Reverend Frogge rolled his eyes heavenward, thankful she was leaving.

It was late when she left, dark several hours, but a full moon was out, and Reverend Frogge could see the shadows it cast. It was all quite lovely, he thought as he watched the Widow Foster leave in her car, the shadows of trees on the road, the stars sparkling above. It was so warm for this time of year. He hardly needed a jacket, he thought, as he grabbed a light one, just in case, throwing it over his shoulder. He would walk down to the witch's house now. She would be alone. Naomi, her daughter, would be at work. No one would see him if he was careful. He looked both ways as he crossed the road. No one coming. He ran until he was safely on the tree-lined road to the witch's house. No one saw him—that was good. He breathed easier, begging his heart to slow its pounding.

He could confront her, demand that she stop this foolish wager, but he knew that wouldn't faze her. He considered escalating into physical intimidation, hitting her, shaking her until she gave. For a moment he admitted to himself how good it would feel to see that kind of fear in Anaya's eyes, but then he remembered how she'd fought with John—and how he'd waddled like a penguin for a week afterwards. Well, that wasn't going to work. Maybe if he begged. No one would see, no one would believe her if she told. But she'd just laugh at him. He knew that.

Reverend Frogge stopped in front of Anaya's house, when Helga, her guard goose, honked at him from her cage in disapproval. He paused, waiting for her to be quiet. In the moonlight, Anaya's house seemed so peaceful, but he knew that was deceptive. He thought about running home, but, no, he had to deal with the wager. Clearing his head, he walked toward the door, stepping lightly on the porch so that it didn't squeak, just in case he chickened out.

Then he remembered the first time he'd come to her house and seen Anaya, all of her. She might be naked again. That wouldn't work, God above, that wouldn't work—him alone with the witch—the nude witch. He had better check to make sure. He looked through the little window in the door, and couldn't see anything but the front room. He lightly walked to some windows further down, around the corner, where he could see into the kitchen, and, sure enough, there she was, awesomely bare, working at the counter, making something. He shook his head in disbelief. God couldn't be this cruel.

He felt himself begin to stiffen, and then get uncomfortably hard. He put his coat down on the floor and sat down on it below the window to peek in better, telling himself he would wait until she put clothes on and could safely answer the door. Unconsciously, he leaned back and reached for his crotch, adjusting his erection so it didn't hurt so much. He looked around. Nobody was there, nobody saw him. What would it hurt? He undid his belt, unzipped his pants, and pulled his pants and his shorts down to his knees, letting his erection bloom out. Slowly, he began to stroke it, completely absorbed by the witch.

When Naomi reached Helga's pen, she noticed movement in the shadows on the corner of the porch. She looked again, trying to see through the night. Yes, someone was there, peeking in through the window at her mother! Outraged, Naomi looked around and found a tree branch that would make a good club. She went to Helga's cage, whispering at her to be quiet. She opened the door to the pen, letting Helga out, and together they stalked the intruder.

So quiet was their approach, and so distracted was the Reverend, that they were well upon him before he sensed anything. Still not seeing who it was, Naomi let out a whoop and charged the last couple of yards, Helga honking furiously ahead of her. When they got to him, Helga went for the Reverend's head while Naomi beat him on the buttocks with the club. Reverend Frogge struggled to run, but fell to his knees, trying to swat Helga away and avoid Naomi's blows. He couldn't pull his pants up with Naomi and Helga attacking him, so he kicked them off, losing his shoes in the process. Free of his pants, he got up and ran, but Helga flew up toward his head and beat him with her wings. He stumbled and fell to the ground, where he got more blows from Naomi and pecks from Helga. Desperately, one hand shielding his head, the other his groin, he got up, and saw a nearby apple tree in bloom, and ran for it, breathing a sigh of relief as he climbed up into it. He was in the upper branches, with Helga and Naomi circling triumphantly below, hurling curses and honks at him, when Anaya turned the porch lights on and came out.

She was wearing a housecoat and carrying a flashlight in one hand and the scourge from her altar in the other. "*What* is going on out here?" she demanded.

"A Peeping Tom was looking in the window. Helga and I treed him," Naomi said, triumphant.

Anaya aimed the flashlight into the tree where they saw Reverend Frogge perched on a branch and desperately trying to cover his groin with his hands. Blinded by the light, he lost his balance and had to grab the tree with both hands, leaving his all-too-persistent erection exposed. Anaya and Naomi gaped for a moment, then finally Anaya shimmied her shoulders, grinned and purred, "Well, *hello* lover."

"This isn't what you think it is," Reverend Frogge protested.

"No, Reverend, it is *exactly* what I think it is," Anaya said, shining the light beam right on his erection. "The evidence is pretty conclusive."

"I came to talk about the wager," he objected, trying to cover himself with one hand. He squirmed around on the branch and with great effort, managed to take his shirt off and use it to cover his lap.

"Uh huh, and you could have just knocked, walked in, and, poof, with that hard-on we would be fucking by now. That would have been so much better, instead of getting Naomi and Helga all wound up." She stepped closer to the tree, smiling suggestively.

"No," he pleaded, "I came to call off the bet. We must end this now."

She seemed to ponder the idea, furrowing her brow in a parody of deep thought. "Now why would I want to do that?"

"It would be the decent thing to do."

Naomi snickered, "Look who's talking about being decent."

This angered him, a mere girl lecturing him. "I could charge you with assault, you Jezebel. You had no grounds for attacking me," he shouted.

Naomi dropped the branch and reached for the scourge held by her mother, who pulled it back from her. "Can I hurt him, Mom? Just a little bit? Please?"

Anaya shook her head disapprovingly. "That's mighty Republican of you. But we'll work this out—without violence." To

Reverend Frogge she said, "Why don't you come down from there? We'll go inside, I'll take off my house coat, and we can discuss your Peeping Tom issues."

Sitting there, imagining what the Widow Foster would say if she found out, Reverend Frogge decided that the best defense was a strong offense. "Cage that Goddamned bird, give me my pants, you fucking whore, and I'll be out of here. I wouldn't fuck you if you were the last woman on earth. You're old, your tits sag, and you probably have a venereal disease."

Anaya blinked, then handed Naomi the scourge. "Don't hurt him too much, dear," she said. "No blood, no broken bones, and be careful with his cock. I want it in good operating condition." She stepped back as Naomi joyously slashed the scourge's whips down on the Reverend's thigh, the tips whistling through the air, snapping loudly when they hit naked flesh. He screamed in pain and struggled to get higher in the tree, dropping his shirt to the ground. Helga honked and flapped her wings, encouraging Naomi on. The girl climbed up on a lower branch of the tree, getting a good swipe at the Reverend's butt, leaving deep red welts. As he climbed higher, she pursued him, the scourge repeatedly whistling through the air, ripping into bare skin. He shrieked each time it hit, finally begging, "Stop it. Please, stop it."

"Apologize to both of us," Naomi said, breathing hard. "And make it good. I'm really getting tired of this Jezebel crap. It pisses me off."

"OK, OK, you're right," he said. "I shouldn't have called you a Jezebel, or your mother a whore. I used utterly inappropriate language, especially for a minister. I won't do it again."

"That's better," Naomi said, climbing down from the tree. "Just make sure you don't change your mind, or I'll be all over your ass with the scourge again."

Anaya picked up Helga, petted her on the head, and cooed, "What a good goose you are, helping my daughter like that."

"His holiness up there claims he's repented, but frankly, Mom, I don't believe him. He's just the same asshole he's always been."

"Maybe, but you were quite persuasive, my fierce Amazonian princess," Anaya said, kissing Naomi on the forehead. "Maybe he's learned something." She handed the goose to Naomi. Could you take Helga and put her back in her pen? Give her some extra feed; she was *such* a good goose. While you take care of her, I'll chat with the newly repentant Reverend here."

"Come on Helga, you probably shouldn't see this," Naomi said, cuddling the goose. "It'll be more than a celibate goose can handle."

As her daughter walked away, Anaya dropped her robe, leaving herself completely naked in the moonlight, and said to Frogge, "Wanna take a bite from my apple, Reverend?"

How It Goes Down

Noel Sloboda

Reasons to stay
     on the wagon
          melt at first

taste of the clear
     hot stuff burning
          your tongue

your throat
     your belly
          finally that thing

that made you
     swallow plans
          to stop.

I Can Almost Taste It

Grāzina Smith

When I first started school I found out that something I've always done was very wrong. The day it happened was damp and drizzly, the fall air thick with my favorite smells of wet earth and moldy leaves. We were running around the school yard, butting and pushing each other, when Billy fell. He tore his elbow on the gravel and sat up, trying not to cry. We stared at the gash on his arm—just starting to ooze warm, red blood. I went over and kneeled down by him, lifted his elbow and licked the wound. When it started to flow, I put my mouth tight around the cut and sucked those precious drops.

I didn't even know Miss Henner was in the yard until she yanked me away from Billy and shook me hard, yelling, "What's wrong with you—you dirty girl? Wait 'til I tell your Ma."

She slapped my face, took me to the bathroom and lathered an old rag with lye soap. Then she scrubbed my mouth and tongue. I didn't say a word, just tried not to swallow or gag. I don't know when she talked to Ma, but she did. A few days later, when I walked in from school, Ma looked up from the carrot she was scraping and said, "Well, I reckon' it be best if you be takin' blood only at home." And that was all. She never said another word about it. That's the thing with Ma—she never tells me if something is right or wrong or if I'm doing something really terrible.

Ma knows how partial I am to blood. After killing a chicken, she always bleeds a tin cup full for me. I stand in the kitchen and sip, letting its sharp, salty taste coat my mouth and roll down my throat, slow, always wishing the cup was magic, bottomless. Once Pa came in while I was drinking, gave us both a hard stare and shook his head.

"That be *your* side," he said nodding at Ma. She was blushing and seemed almost trembling for a minute.

Then Ma squared her shoulders and answered, "She just be needing it...like Great-Aunt Eulah." Pa shrugged and left the kitchen.

"Great-Aunt Eulah? Who's Eulah?" I asked. Ma didn't answer. "Where'd she live?" Ma pursed her lips and shook her head. "She be gone."

"But where'd she go?" I asked.

"Away," and Ma picked up the hogs' slop bucket and went out the door. I kept my ears open to see if Eulah would be mentioned again and even spent many evenings sitting on the floor near the front door, pretending to play with my rag doll, while Ma and my big sister Mary sat on the porch, quilting or shelling beans or peas. Seemed like they gossiped about everybody in the holler, but Eulah's name never came up.

Ma cossets me—my need for blood, I mean. When she fries a rabbit, she always puts my piece in last—at the far side of the iron skillet—so it never cooks through. I bite into the warm chunk until I hit bone and can taste the raw meat and the bloody drops. I draw the liquid out, chewing slow and sucking until the meat goes pulpy in my mouth. I don't like to swallow it and try to sneak it back on the side of my plate. If Mary sees, she screws up her face and grumbles: "Stop! Eat that meat like the rest of us." But she knows I'm not like the rest of them.

When I lower my eyes and peer through my lashes at the family around the table, I can see how different I am from them. I'm almost 13, and even though Mary's only two years older, she's tall as Ma and can wear Ma's dresses. When they're together, with their backs to me, I can hardly tell one from the other. They both have thick, black hair curling to their shoulders. Their skin's a soft gold, the same shade as the feathers on our bantam hens, and the muscles on their arms stand out like knobs on a hickory limb.

Pa's a coal miner and looks like a man who spends his life underground. His face is powdered with gray coal dust that seems to seep through his skin into his flesh. His bushy eyebrows tangle down and dark stains go all around his eyes making it look like he's staring at us from out of a cave.

I'm small, thin and pale. When I hold up my homework for Miss Henner, my hands are so white I can hardly tell where my fingers end and the paper begins. Ma says my hair is like a halo, but the kids at school nicknamed me "Dandelion." My light, wispy hair springs out from my head like Dandy-Lion seed puffs. I'm strong, though, and do my share. I clean, cook, and chop wood, too, and got no trouble hefting those fifty-pound bags of flour Ma brings from the store. But everything I do has to be done inside the house or in deep shade.

I cannot stay in sunlight. When I was very small, Mary took me out to the meadow to pick wild flowers and we danced around in the warm spring sunshine. That night I got so sick, Ma sure thought I'd die. My body was fever-hot and my skin got all red where the sun had got me through my thin cotton dress. My face, arms and legs were covered with large raw blisters that broke open and wouldn't stop leaking. Ma wrapped me in sheets soaked in chamomile and hyssop and put chickweed and oatmeal poultices on my sores. It was days before I got back to normal, and Ma still warns me I can't never play in the sun. I don't. Those burns hurt strong in my memory.

I stay indoors except for the gloomiest days and walk to school through the shady parts of the forest, then run across the yard and shut myself in the classroom. School's almost finished and I won't have to worry about it much longer. The other kids are full of plans, but not me. Mary's being courted by the Taggert boy and I guess, in a few years, I'll have to find someone to marry and get a house of my own—and maybe children. If I ask Ma anything about it, she always says, "Hush, child. It be too soon. No need worryin' your head about any of that yet." I try talking to her today, but she grabs a small pail and pushes me out the door, saying, "It be a good day for you to find some berries—reckon' we can make a pie."

I know it's too early for ripe berries, but it's a perfect day for me. It rained all night and even though it stopped, the day's so cloudy it's dark as dusk. There's a mist weaving in and out of the trees and nearly covering the path up the hill. It's good to be out of the house, and soon I find a bush with raspberries. I carefully plunk the few ripe ones into the pail. The ground is soft under my feet and my toes sink in as I strain to reach the ripe berries—guess that's why I don't hear Billy come up the hill 'til he's right by me. He's always hanging around and grinning at me. He likes to be called "Big Bill" now that he's tall. His Adam's apple juts out and jiggles every time he talks—usually bragging about working in the mine soon. I think of Pa and know that's nothing to boast about.

"H...Hi," he mumbles. "What cha doin'?"

"Picking berries. Can't you see? Ma wants to make a pie but there not be enough ripe to do that," I answer.

"Here—I'll help you," and he starts to pull every berry off that bush. He throws them into the pail by the handful.

"We can't use those." I look down at the mess of hard, green berries in my pail.

"W..w...why not?" He turns. Sweat's shiny all over his forehead. I look down at his calloused fingers, streaked red from the few ripe berries he managed to pick and crush. Between his thumb and pointer finger, in that soft fleshy part, is a drop of blood. A thorn must have pricked him. I watch it swell–round and fat with a deep, dark color and I wet my lips. Billy's talking but I don't hear him. I'm lost in that cherry red bead. I take his hand up to my mouth, real slow, and suck the cut.

Suddenly, Billy grips my waist with his free arm, pulls me into him and buries his face in my neck—moaning and mumbling and slobbering kisses near my ear. I try to pull away, but he yanks his hand from my lips and lifts me off my feet. He begins to stroke and knead the small bumps that are my breasts. I twist and turn trying to loosen his hold, but he presses harder against me, his leg pushing between mine, and kicking the pail over into the mud. Finally, I stop struggling and he holds me close; his warm breath blows into my ear. I raise my hands to his chest, stiffen, and with a great push, I send him toward the berry brambles. He doesn't expect that, and the slick ground gives way under his feet. Billy crashes down, arms and legs thrashing in the raspberry canes. I grab my empty pail from the ground and run down the path not turning to see how far he falls.

My breath's all steady by the time I get home. I swing the pail on to the kitchen table and before she can ask me, I tell Ma, "I ate the ripe berries. There not be enough for pie." She nods her head and turns back to the stove.

That night at the table, my stomach churns and gurgles and feels like I've swallowed a bucket of worms. I can't eat a bite and push the catfish and corn bread around my plate crumbling the food into small heaps. "You better eat them fish," Mary says. "Fred caught 'em and brought 'em for Ma to cook. That be so nice of him." She smiles a silly smile.

"Fred Taggert only brought 'em over 'cause he's sweet on you." I snap. "He don't care what we eat." Mary shakes her head but I can tell she's pleased with him.

My belly's all swollen up like I drunk a whole pitcher of water, with some kind of sharp pains coming and going inside me. "Ma, I gotta lay down. I don't feel so good."

"Did you eat a lot of them green berries?" Ma asks.

"No...no." I push away from the table. I'm not sure she believes me.

In my room, I get into my nightgown and curl up in bed to hug my sore belly. Memories of this afternoon tease at me and my heart thumps fast and strong. I remember Billy gripping me, and a shiver runs all down my spine. My body tingles like a giant bubble's filling my chest and going to burst inside me. I smell the sour sweat of his red flannel shirt and the sweet hay in his hair all over again. I'm all mixed up and feel like I want to tell Mary I could've almost died when he held me.

From overhearing Ma talk to Mary, I know that a man has to get close to you to make a baby, and when that happens, your belly swells up. Billy held me so close that a handful of pine needles wouldn't fit between us. Did he make a baby in me? I can't ask Ma and I twist and turn, my belly hurting, my mind thrashing like a squirrel in a cage.

Later on, Ma comes into my room with a towel she's warmed in the oven and a big cup of blackberry leaf tea.

"Here–drink this. There be honey and whiskey in the tea, and lay that warm towel on your belly," she says. "Now if you be needin' me, just holler."

The towel and the sweet, strong tea loosen my body and I drift off to sleep. It's dawn when I open my eyes. I can hear Ma in the kitchen starting breakfast and hope she's making something special for me. My belly feels better, but when I press on it with my hand, something warm and sticky spurts out between my legs. My bed is damp. I put my hand down there and bring my fingers up to the morning light. A dark red smear shines across my fingers and I smell a sharp odor like old blood left in the sun. Why's this coming out of me? Will I bleed until I die? I can't ask Ma. She never talks to me about my thirst for blood. How can I tell her this terrible thing's happening to me? I stare at my stained fingers and bring them to my lips, real slow.

⋮

138

⋮

What Lurks at Midnight
Nancy Sparks

Quarter to midnight—I knew, having checked at least a dozen times. Katie, my office mate, intently studied the papers before her, head down. Our project was due at nine the next morning, and if we wanted to keep our jobs, it had to get done.

Working late was always a bitch, but those murders since December had really put us both on edge. The last poor woman had been duct-taped, shot, carved up with a knife and dumped in a supply closet like all the others. Even with police running beefed-up patrols, we knew we weren't safe from this lunatic who preyed on women in offices, late at night. Who knew what compelled such serial killers? Broken genes? Faulty parenting? Avidly, I followed every development, heart pounding but unable to stop reading about the victims, their wounds...unable to change the channel, and for the first time, joining those who are somehow drawn to such horrors.

Sighing, I straightened up and stretched and froze as I sensed a movement down the darkened hall. Katie's head was still down, focused on the figures in front of her. I leaned forward over my desk, trying to see further down the hall.

"Shit, shit, shit," she muttered under her breath, "These numbers don't add up. I need chocolate."

She must have noticed my silence, because she looked at me and said "What's wro...." her voice dropped off when a scraping sound from down the hall interrupted her.

We both stared down the hall. Katie's hand crept toward her telephone; mine grabbed the letter opener lying on my desk. We held our breath and waited for the sound to reoccur, but there was silence.

"You gonna go look?" I whispered, my gaze glued to the hall.

"No, I'm not going out there!"

"One of us has to." I quietly rolled my chair back, stood up and moved to the office door. Taking a breath, I flipped on the lights, illuminating the short hallway and lobby, with its entrance from the parking lot. I thought I heard a small thud by the outside door, but I couldn't be sure. Letter opener clutched in my sweating hand, I crept down the hallway past the open bathroom door on my left and peered around the corner into the lobby.

Nothing.

I moved to the outside door; it was locked. Cautiously I looked out into the parking lot.

"I don't see anything out here," I called to Katie, flipped the lights off and started back to our office.

Suddenly a dark shape darted out of the bathroom and ran down the hall, straight at Katie! I screamed and raced back into the lobby. Katie echoed my scream and jumped up onto her chair, then onto her desk, sending her chair and stacks of paper flying.

"Oh God, oh God," Katie kept repeating.

"Where did it go?" I had finally recovered my wits enough to look back down the hall.

"Under my desk!" Katie shrieked. "Get it!" Katie was terrified of mice. She reminded me of one of those cartoon elephants that fainted at the sight of a mouse.

"I'll try to catch it." I rooted around in the lobby and came up with a plastic coffee can, just the right size to hold the wild beast.

"Stay up there while I look around." I carefully picked up the scattered papers and peered around her overturned chair. I spotted the little gray field mouse crouched next to her file cabinet.

"I see him," I said quietly, "Don't move."

Lowering the coffee can, I maneuvered until it was about twelve inches from the quivering little thing, then took a file folder and moved it behind the mouse, trying to herd him into the can.

The mouse had other ideas. He jumped up and onto the coffee can, ran over my hand and back down the hall into the bathroom.

I dropped the can and jumped back as Katie started hyperventilating.

"Calm down!" I picked up the coffee can and came back around her desk. "He went into the bathroom. I think we can trap him in there."

"We? You're kidding, right?" Katie's blue eyes widened with disbelief.

"No, you need to come down here and help me trap this thing."

Katie slowly stepped down from her desk and came to the hallway.

"I think I see him back in the corner." The poor creature sat next to the toilet, sides heaving, probably as terrified as we were. "I can probably catch him this time. You stand out here and if he tries to come out shoo him back in. We can do this." I gave her a hard stare.

"OK, OK, just get him."

I walked into the bathroom, coffee in one hand, file folder in another. Bent low, I slowly approached the mouse. His gaze darted back and forth between me and the door, as if trying to figure out the best route of escape. I moved the can closer, closer, and suddenly he made his move. He feigned left, then darted right as I tried to follow his movements, but I wasn't quick enough. He ran between my legs and headed straight at Katie, who let out a squawk. This seemed to momentarily confuse the mouse, and as I spun around I saw Katie jump up in the air. The disoriented mouse made a sharp turn and darted back toward our office, the same direction Katie jumped. Her foot came down, landing on the mouse's tail, which started him squeaking and lunging around. Katie leapt off the mouse's tail and ran toward the lobby. The mouse, tail dragging, ran in a circle before hading the opposite direction toward our office. I jumped out in the hallway and watched Katie as she apparently decided she'd had enough of being in the same building as the mouse. She ran toward the parking lot exit and flung the heavy, steel door outward with such force that it struck something, making a loud thud. I had started toward the door when she came running back into the building.

"Call the police! There's a man outside and I hit him with the door!"

I grabbed the phone and dialed 911. We huddled behind Katie's desk as I gave the operator our names and location. Less than three minutes passed before we heard the sirens, went to the window and watched as two squad cars and an ambulance raced in. The police drew their guns and surrounded the man, who still lay unconscious by the door, blood running down his bald scalp. They handcuffed him and the paramedics carried him away in an ambulance.

The police sergeant came in the office to take our statements about what had happened. I could see him trying to keep a straight face as I described the mouse incident, but he turned serious.

"You ladies are very lucky. We found a gun, a knife and duct tape on him."

Katie and both gasped, staring at each other, as his words sunk in. We'd been the next intended victims of the serial killer.

While the police were still working I returned to my desk to find our little mouse still dazed, huddling in the corner by my desk. I took the coffee can and quickly scooped him up, snapping on the lid.

As the police were leaving, I glanced at Katie, who was sitting at her desk looking into space.

"The hell with the project," I muttered, "I could really use a drink."

We headed over to my condo, where I dragged out my blender and fixed us something really strong. While Katie sat stiffly on the overstuffed couch and clutched a double strawberry margarita, I headed to the basement for an old fish tank and some screen. I carried them upstairs and set them on the coffee table in front of her. Pulling the coffee can out from behind the couch where I'd left it, I dumped the mouse into the tank and covered it with the screen. Only the tiny sound of the mouse's nails scratching at the glass broke the silence. Apparently not repulsed, Katie took a sip of her drink, gravely regarding the little gray creature, and her hunched shoulders slackened as she leaned back into the cushions.

The Cold Wet Campus

Greg Stolze

Schroeder was just starting to masturbate when he heard the knock on his door. "Hold on!" he shouted, pulling up his sweatpants, glad he hadn't yet opened his lotion. He took a deep breath, paused the stereo, and unlocked the door. He only opened it half-way, peeking around it and standing behind.

He blinked when he saw Jayden standing behind an elderly woman in a wheelchair. "Schroeder man, I needjer help."

"Um?"

"Mrs. Denabli here got caught out in the rain, Davis brought her to the dorm and she's, like, totally chilled. Your room's right over the furnace, I know it's always super hot in here, can she, like, come in and warm up?"

"Um…" Schroeder blinked.

"Thanks, dude. You're a lifesaver." Jayden started pushing the wheelchair against the door and, unwilling to blatantly block it, Schroeder let her in. Jayden didn't even cross the threshold. "It won't be too long, I know you gotta study and stuff, but she's totally stuck. We're looking for her nephew right now."

"Wait, you're not…?" Schroeder blinked again, rapidly.

"Sorry, dude, got to ramble on. Looking for her ride, y'know? Back real soon."

Then the door was closed and they were alone.

"Uh… hi," Schroeder said.

"I'm terribly sorry if this is an imposition," the woman replied.

"Oh, nah, nothing… I mean, if I can't help out a… you know. It's no big deal. You want me to put some coffee on the hotplate or something?"

"That other young man… Jason?"

"Jayden."

"He gave me a little something to warm me up," she said. Schroeder furrowed his brow. Her voice was coy. In fact, she even giggled a bit.

"Okay." He sat on the bed, trying to casually cross his legs to conceal his still painfully urgent erection.

"You know, in my day, college boys weren't allowed to have liquor in the dorms," she said, adjusting one of the wheels.

"We still aren't."

"Oh my! Well, I won't tell about Jayden if you won't."

"How'd you get stuck in the rain?"

She sighed. "My nephew Blake teaches a class here, and we were going out for my birthday. I was waiting in the library—it's nice to get out sometimes, you know. I looked out the window and saw someone at his car, so I went out thinking it was him. But it was this other boy, David I guess."

"Davis."

"He said he was trying to fix Blake's window, which wouldn't close, and then the two of us went into the library and waited such a long time, and Blake didn't come back. Your friend Davis had somewhere he had to be, so he insisted that I come here. Poor fellow, he didn't want to abandon me in the library. Everyone's been very sweet." She giggled again. "That doesn't look very comfortable."

"Excuse me?"

She gestured at his lap.

Schroeder instantly turned crimson and spun away. This time she laughed out loud.

"Sorry," he muttered.

"Oh, no, don't be, don't be embarrassed. I'm sure you'll make some woman very happy with that someday." Even through his humiliation, he could hear a tone of... regret? Wistfulness?

"Yeah, uh, you're too kind," he said, still facing away from her. But in the window's reflection, he could see her wheeling closer.

"Listen young man, if it's staying at attention like a marine at a funeral, even when you're surprised and uncomfortable... well, I've said too much." She paused, then added, "Especially when a woman with a cataract on one eye can spot it from across the room."

"Well, it's a small room," Schroeder said, and then gasped. He looked down. A slender, veiny hand had grasped him through his pants. He looked at her with his mouth open in shock and was even more surprised to see tears welling in her eyes.

"I'm sorry," she said, with a sniff. "I just... it's been so long since I've seen a man's body. And they're so beautiful."

"Miss..."

"My name's Emily." She dabbed a tear with her other hand and gave a rueful smile. "I'm probably being too familiar when we haven't been introduced."

Schroeder opened his mouth and then shut it again because, despite her bashful words, her hand was moving with a confident expertise. She looked up at him and tilted her head to the side. "You want me to go on. Don't you?"

"Uh..."

"It's all right. It's like Jason and his whiskey. I won't tell if you won't." Her smile took on a wicked aspect as she said, "I'm well past the age of consent."

"This just seems wrong." He managed to get it out, then blinked hard as a second busy hand joined the first.

"Wrong?"

"Like I'm taking advantage of you."

"Mr. Schroeder, I know what I'm doing. Would it surprise you to know I made a dirty movie once?"

He took another sharp breath and said, "Actually, no."

"Please," she said. "Slip that shirt off. Make an old woman happy."

Schroeder didn't know what to do. In the absence of any rational alternative, he followed the path of least resistance.

"So wonderful," she sighed. Then she said, "Just a moment," slipped out her false teeth and leaned closer. "You can close your eyes and think of someone else," she said coquettishly. "I won't mind."

So there Schroeder stood, pants down and shut-eyed by her wheelchair, as the door swung open and his roommate Tyler barged in. In the distance, thunder rolled.

———†——†———

Hours later, the rain had trailed off and the sun was setting under an eyebrow of low clouds. Blake Cassidy cleared his throat as he pulled his car up in front of the retirement home. "Again, Aunt Em, I'm sorry this turned into..." He trailed off as he got out to open the car door for her. "I mean... if you're disappointed..."

"Blake dear, I had a lovely time."

"Well, I really wanted to take you to Casa Del Monica..." Gently he eased her into her wheelchair and opened an umbrella over her head, just in case.

"I'm not fancy," she said. "I enjoyed the pancake house just as much. And I got a lovely visit of the campus where you teach."

"Hm. A cold, wet visit."

She laughed before continuing. "Besides, you did the right thing. If that poor girl was injured you certainly had to take care of her."

"Ugh, I hope that doesn't turn into a huge stink."

"You said she signed a waiver when she signed up for... for... what is it you teach again?"

"Tae Kwon Do," he said, frowning. "But I'm just worried the college won't ask me back."

"Sufficient unto the day are the concerns thereof," Emily said with kind piety. Blake kissed her cheek.

"Happy seventy-ninth, Aunt Emily."

"It was certainly that."

He nodded to the attendant at her nursing home, who smiled back as she wheeled Emily within.

"You have a nice visit?" the aide asked, her voice mild and distracted.

"I gave the French pleasures to two college boys!"

"That's nice."

Back at the dorm, Schroeder lay on the top bunk staring at the ceiling. "We're going to hell."

"What're you beefing about?" Tyler asked from below.

"What we did was wrong, Tyler. Wrong on many levels."

"Dude, we dirty double-teamed a *porn star*." He grinned. "That, in my book, is *right* on many levels."

"A porn star from the 1950s!"

"I didn't even know they *had* porno back then."

"Did you overlook the wheelchair, Tyler?"

"What, disabled people don't need love too? We made an old woman happy. *Really* happy." His grin widened. "From what I could tell, she made you pretty damn happy too."

"Oh, like you weren't the one moaning and gasping and saying 'Yes —please. Oh more—please. A little faster, *please*.' C'mon!"

"I'm not ashamed of it," Tyler said. "Usually, when a guy says a woman was begging for it and was grateful afterwards, he's frontin' or trying to justify something, but we got this, you know, this *very experienced* woman and she was totally into it. Man," he said, shaking his head in amazement, "you've been in a threeway! Most guys go their whole lives dreaming of a threeway and never get the chance!"

"I don't think most guys imagine a *ménage a trois* with their roommate and a woman who has her false teeth out."

Tyler made a sound of deep disgust. "Christ, Schroeder, talk about your glass half empty. You could ruin a free lunch."

"She probably has senile dementia."

"*You* probably have *penile* dementia. I mean, who'd we hurt? No one. Whose business is it, what we do behind closed doors? Nobody's."

"I feel like I took advantage. Like I... did something I wanted to never do." Schroeder shifted uncomfortably in his bunk.

"What, you took an oath of senior celibacy? You got a promise ring and one of those chastity contracts?" He paused for emphasis. "With a special clause 'bout getting your cob huffed by the elderly?"

"Hey, shut up!"

Tyler didn't. "You're just suffering blowback from all kinds of wack social programming that tells you you can't be sexual with anyone who doesn't look like Elisha Cuthbert. Grow beyond it! College is '*sposta* be a time of expanding yer horizons."

Schroeder just groaned.

"Look, I took an ethics course last quarter, so I know what I'm talking about when I say *it's all good*," Tyler insisted.

"Didn't you get an Incomplete in that course?"

"Right, I'm gone." Tyler rolled off his bunk, pulled on jeans, and was out the door before Schroeder could speak.

———⊥———

That night, Tyler found a underground dub band performance and wound up crashing on the bass player's sofa at four in the morning.

Schroeder tossed and turned and didn't sleep a wink.

Emily Denabli slept longer and more soundly than she had in two years.

Handle with Care
Carla Stout

The blush tulips on the table
are turning out, explicitly curling
around their hothouse sex. And I
think they are more strange
and velvet now than in crystal
vase. I refrain from touching
them in this fragile state for fear
I would drain them of their pearl
petals destined for coarse oak

grain. And if I pick raspberries,
I must take care for a slip
of the wrist will unravel the fruit
twisting it from the vine. If I
serve red wine, I must release
the cork without a trace and let it
breathe to unlace its torpidity. You

come without warning labels,
without alarms, bite, sting, fallout
or screams. I must handle you
with care. Treat you like a found
cobra's egg and unleash you like
a fledgling raven. Lay you in a nest
of mink scorpions and tether you
with satin lizard garrote. I must

be so gentle with you, serving you
lotus and absinthe, enough to keep
you languorous and happy but barely
breathing.

Given Warmth
Darian Stout

I saw my first robin
as it was eating the love cake you made me.
Its brown polished chest
almost too perfect to have been weaned
from the nip of recent winter.
Not long enough of a quench
to forever engage its bobbing face
but a reminder to the beak
that savors this small promise
of spring's vital sugar.

Two days later, in the shadow of a budding maple,
a frozen rabbit is questionably alive.
The cake, nears its head, further gnawed
by the beaks of those early returned.
I too may endure the grasp of his fur,
if only this sudden heat would enter.

Eden's Bar & Grill

Lynn Tait

I don' wanna upset you or anythin',
but there's a snake in yur hair
looks mighty hungry.
He's got one eye on you,
one on me—
this ain't no match made in heaven.
Jus' sit still. Reeel quiet like.
Think cold thoughts.
Maybe, it'll loosen its grip,
sidewind t'ords someone else's garden.
Jus' don' make any sudden moves.
I've seen his type before—
always yappin' bout improvin' yurself,
tryin' to make ya eat sumpthin'
when yur not even hungry—
givin' ya all this nutrition'l bs
bout fruit—how it's good fur ya.
Hell, I don' even like fruit!
So be reeel still.
If I kin sneak up behind and grab 'im—
he'll make good eatin'!

The Showdown
Marilyn L. Taylor

Okay, Zucchini,
with your sleek Sicilian good looks—
I know all about you and the rest
of the Zucca family, how you start out
small, in the corner of some
respectable old *giardino* (nobody
even notices) and then you spread,
don't you, till you've moved in on
all the little guys, the beans
and the carrots and cukes,
and pretty soon you're in charge
of the whole damn *fattoria*, right?
Well, I've got news for you, pal,
you're past your prime. You're ripe
to spend the rest of your natural life
in the cooler. Think I'm kidding?
Listen, either play along or it's
Ratatouille! Ratatouille!
—a year in the jug for you, Zuke.
And your little tomato, too.

Studying the Menu
Marilyn L. Taylor

Speaking of all those things you'll never eat,
my love—could one of them, in fact, be crow?
Of course it could. But you already know
how poisonous it tastes (if bittersweet).
These days you're craving quite another treat:
the one who will replace me. But that sloe-
eyed, slack-jawed creature's surely going to show
you all the nuance of a bitch in heat.

I hope she has the brains of a golden retriever,
the glamour of an aging manatee,
the refinement of a Packers wide receiver
and finds her favorite books at Dollar Tree.
—And darling, may she be a born deceiver,
and do to you what you have done to me.

To the Man Who Says He Doesn't Dream at Night

Judith Valente

He closes his eyes, drifts off
    on an inflatable raft of theta brain waves.

The pons taps out a Morse code
    to the thalamus, cerebral cortex.

Neurons surge through circuitry
    dense enough to under-gird

the city of Washington. They arc, flame,
    and go blank.

He does not ride the back fender
    of a taxicab across a sea of urine,

or rise up on a geyser to grab an airplane wing
    mid-air with his bare hand,

or suffer the panic of the door that will not lock
    to the dark house, where lizards

drip off the tips of a spider plant.
    He does not walk barefoot in slush,

forgetting the spot he's parked the car,
    or sip chamomile with dead aunts

at the flowered ironing board table.
    He wakes to sunlight

seeping through beechwood branches,
    notes in Cyrillic script

on the blank page of his bedroom wall:
    white handwriting of morning.

Once Touched by the Wolf
Claudia Van Gerven

There is no going back. She gave away
the red cape and the basket of useless food.

She cut the pelt into a stunning jacket, wore it with skin tight

Lycra, the same menacing shade
of gray-blue. She began to rout

through singles bars, sniffing out
pretty boys with keen teeth—

and a twitch in their jeans. She drove them
into wooded night, ravening with hunger.

She licked the fine down on the tips
of their ears as they stared speechless

into her fathomless yellow eyes.
She woke each morning

with a furred tongue, watched
her grandmother's stoic face

etch itself
across her mirror, let water
from the shower head stream

across a belly,
smooth and heavy
as stone.

Forcing Spring
Claudia Van Gerven

I amble after some unadvertised want
vaguely behind my metal cart down the aisles
at the Safeway. Then I recognize it:

hieratic bulb wrapped in a scab of reticence
among Muzak & dying bouquets.

Five ninety-nine
and I own it, can rip away
the cardboard sleeve with its instructions
and Dutch promises of hyacinths.

I fill a drainage tray with clean
pebbles, place   the visitant on the sill
between sun and dishwasher, insist

five purple legates unfurl
from green refusal, this fist so taciturn I know I will

have to wrestle this angel, pry each knuckle
loose with water   vigilance,   nitrogen

until the word for blue spice blesses me,
until a sentence of sharp stars
claws my brown skin open.

Billie
Stella Vanapoulos

You flash the smile
Teeth all white, sharp and glistening,
Wet with want above the star spangles
of sequins that shimmy, shimmy, shimmy.

The white gardenia nods and bobs
at faces shining in this dark, massed crowd.
The light, white as your gardenia,
shines brightly on your form.

Sure, you eye the room,
sure in your silky dress,
sure in your little shimmy

in the stage light strobe so right for sequins.

Your soaring notes above the wail of sax
sing of better times, lost times, times to come.
The melody curls in, deep in,
into jazz roots of black and blue.

Eyes bright and seeking, you scan the club through shadows,
finding doorways to the safety of the dark grace beyond
while your white gardenia
nods and bobs. You see it all.

He Says
Dianalee Velie

He says he lost his twenties: chewed up
by medical school and internship.
He says he belongs to the clean plate club,
enjoying everything put on his dish.

He says he'd like to see me again.

I am absorbing our conversation,
like polish on tarnished silver,
as the talk shifts to quantum physics
and the power of the observer.

I observe my heart tinkering with trust,
something I had misplaced long ago.
On guard, I ask if he is married.
His answer: Yes, is that a problem?

It is, and it is not, simultaneously.
We have encountered only this event,
solid and substantial with unexplored
variants waiting behind closed doors.

So I slide him to a safe distance, like
the piece of chocolate decadence cake,
after I have devoured three tempting mouthfuls,
regretfully pushing my plate across the table,

still craving so much more.

⋮

156

⋮

The Town That Ate the Chef: A Food Fable
James C. Wall

Pary Newduhl loved food. As a short, pudgy, overweight boy of nine he'd stood in the kitchen one afternoon staring up at a newly baked pie his mother had placed on top of the refrigerator. Even from behind, you could tell as he stared up at all those delicious calories, he was willing that pie to fall down into his eager, open mouth. From the doorway opposite, Grandpa Newduhl snapped a photo of Pary and it later became a famous print. You may have seen it. It's a wonder that neither Weight Watchers nor Jenny Craig snapped up the rights to it to use as their poster child.

Pary went right from high school to culinary school and upon receiving his diploma, told his parents he wanted to open his own cooking school. "I need your money," he informed his parents, Bootsie and Ira Newduhl. "Don't eat all the profits," his father had warned him.

Pary found a small business location for rent a few blocks from the heart of downtown. Because all the new wiring wasn't complete, Pary got a good but still expensive deal, and he signed a two-year lease. "Pary's Special Delights: Cooking Academy" he named it and the Monday afternoon the workers hung the sign was the proudest day of his life. "What's it look like?" Bootsie asked from her Monday afternoon mahjongg table. "The lettering is Roast Beef Gravy brown," he explained into his cell, "On a field of homemade, somewhat lumpy, mashed potatoes–off white! It just makes your mouth water!" he explained to Bootsie. "Don't eat the sign," she advised. Pary went inside and whipped up a Boston Cream Pie and ate half of it in celebration. Now all he needed was students.

Two weeks after that monumental Monday sign hanging, Pary still had no students. He begged his parents for more money. "I need to advertise." he told them. "You need to lose weight!" Bootsie Newduhl told him. So, with even more Newduhl capital, Pary took out ads in the local papers, had flyers sent out, and even paid for some radio spots on which he sang (totally off key) "Here's my Boston Cream Pie— How do you like me so far?"

His first three students signed up at the end of that week. First was Frank Oldman, just recently fired from his bathroom designing job at Lowe's for being a bit too bombastically egotistical. Next was Di Di Gunther, just recently plopped onto the unemployment line amid rumors hinting at an embarrassing bit of company slush fund embezzlement. And finally there was Billy Swade, just recently released from Juvie Hall under a judicial admonishment that he should find a career path that did not involve the words "dope," "doobie," or "drugs." Pary's Special Delights: Cooking Academy was rolling!

All his students loved their new school and Pary their enthusiastic teacher. "More heat!" he advised. "More sugar!" he exclaimed. "More frosting!" he extolled during week three when he sidestepped his own curriculum and delved into the delicious delights of desserts, his lifetime fascination. And things seemed to be going well until his rent came due at the end of that month. I'm short many, many hundreds of dollars, he told himself. But he knew Ma and Pa Newduhl would be of no help. He'd been to that well too many times already. He needed more students and more tuition dollars, he told himself as he labored over the Duck's Blood Soup he was preparing for that day's Ethnic Cuisine class. Week Four was soups and as Pary worried about his electric bill, his water bill, his gas bill, and his rent, his paring knife slipped. "Ouch" he yelled as a small slice of his little finger on his left hand plopped into the soup mixture. He grabbed for it, but only succeeded in dripping a couple of tablespoons of blood into the pot.

"Darn it!" he thought. "Now I've got to throw this out!" "Darn it" he thought, "I can't afford to waste all this soup!" "Darn it" he thought, "Let's just use it and hope to God the taste isn't that bad."

Frank, Di Di, and Billy arrived for class a short time later and they all sampled the Duck's Blood Soup. "I could not have done better myself!" proclaimed bombastic Frank. "I just love it!" cooed the suddenly seductive Di Di who had developed a crush on the teacher. "Dude!" shouted Billy with soup dripping from his mouth.

By the end of the week, the three students had told enough of their friends and acquaintances that Pary's student body had increased to ten. But then the enthusiasm as well as the money leveled off as they entered Week Six—Salads and Veggies. The greens didn't translate into any monetary green and Pary was worried again. He stood at his head of the class counter teaching the art of cutting sausages for Week Seven— Dogs and Brats...Kings of the Backyard Barbecue. "Ouch!" Pary yelled as he absentmindedly cut off three fingers of his left hand that had just started to heal. He grabbed for them just as his students entered the academy kitchen, anxious for their lesson in gourmet grilling. Stuffing his bleeding hand into a balled-up towel, Pary started shouting instructions. He couldn't risk letting his students see his digital mishap. "We've got two hours to get this done, people. Let's get a move on!" He ran to the bathroom to change towels and upon his return, discovered his cut up sausages and fingers were gone. The smell of grilling started to fill the room as his students took to their lesson with passion and panache. Finally they covered their dogs and brats with the secret, soon-to-be-famous Pary Special Delight sauce. A hungry ravenous look appeared on the faces of his students as their grilling lesson came to an end. Then they ate. "Fantastic!" they all raved. "Crunchy! Dude!" yelled Billy.

The next morning, Bootsie and Ira called. "We need all our money back," demanded Ira. "The mortgage has come due on the house," explained Bootsie. "Ma...Pa—where can I find money like that?" Pary whined as he used his good hand to page thru the latest edition of *Cooking Monthly*. Then suddenly, there it was! A full page advertisement from the Sheep Ranchers Association of America. A $10,000 first prize for the best Leg of Lamb. The contest was three days away on Friday at a local downtown hotel. "Leg of Lamb" Pary thought to himself. Leg of Lamb...could this be the answer?

On the following Monday, Pary's students were amazed at the versatility and wide range of options they discovered as they paged thru the various prosthetics catalogues that Pary had absent-mindedly left laying around the counter sink area of the classroom. "This is the best one!" judged bombastic Frank pointing to a shiny wooden leg in his catalogue. "This one is much sexier!" sighed Di Di ogling an aluminum die cast leg in her catalogue. "Dude! Titanium!" shouted Billy as he eyed the prosthetics centerfold in the catalogue he was holding. "Time for class!" yelled Pary as he wheeled himself into the room sitting in his newly rented ("Take it for a test sit" the salesman had said) three-speed, power steering, electric wheel chair. Bootsie and Ira had just called to say how much they loved and appreciated their son. "Lose some weight," Bootsie had said as she hung up the phone.

"Anybody know where Rudolfo and Riva are today?" yelled Pary above the din of mix-masters as he took attendance at the start of class. All eyes looked away, a bit nervous. Perplexed, Pary guided his wheelchair up the aisle in between two lines of students working at their counters. Sticking out of the back pocket of bombastic Frank's work pants was a bold colored orange flyer and as he rolled by, Pary thought he saw the words "cooking school" across the top. He inexpertly threw his wheelchair in reverse, bumped his stump of a left leg into Di Di, who squealed delightedly. "What's this?" Pary screamed, snatching the flyer from Frank's back pocket. "Oh – uh – oh – well..." Frank non-bombastically stuttered. By then Pary had unfolded the flyer and found an announcement for a brand new state of the art cooking school opening up that week across town. "New ovens, new recipes, new chef hats!" the flyer proudly proclaimed. Pary looked at Frank and Di Di and Billy. "Rudolfo? Riva?" he asked. His three oldest students shook their head yes.

I need some brownies, Pary thought as he retreated to his office. As he devoured a second tin of the chocolate delights, he marveled at the calming effect sugar and cocoa beans had on him. With his one good hand, he started to page thru the newly delivered edition of *Cooking Monthly*, pausing to hold up the centerfold (an ear of corn fresh from the steamer, its golden kernels drowning in melted butter), when an envelope fell from between the pages. The return address was "The Cordon Bleu Cooking School Association of America." I've already paid my dues, Pary thought as he opened the letter. But it wasn't about dues. The most famous name in cooking schools was announcing a school cook-off contest! The winning school would receive the wildly coveted Cordon Bleu Gold Ribbon of Excellence! Nothing could be as important to a cooking school as winning recognition like this. "The new school across town will eat my drippings," Pary muttered aloud as he filled out the application, sealed the envelope, and placed a stamp on it. "Pary's Special Delights Cooking Academy will win this award if it's the last thing I ever do," Pary swore.

When told they were being entered in a cooking contest, his students balked. "We're not ready!" said Frank. "We're not that good!" said Di Di. "Dude!" said Billy. "Not to worry," Pary explained. "I'll do all the actual cooking and we'll just put your names on it. All the best schools do it this way." Excited about the contest and the fame it could bring their school, they agreed.

He had one week to get ready. One week to plan his menu. One week to gather his ingredients and one week to prepare his strategy! And at the end of that week, on Friday evening next, the judges for the Cordon Bleu Society would show up, sample his delights, and make their decision. Pary had already been informed that 25 other schools had entered and his school would be the last to be judged on the last night.

Pary's students were thrilled, tense and brimming with pride when they showed up at school on Friday night. "Of course we will win!" Frank bombastically proclaimed. "No one can touch us." "Maybe we should come up with a school cheer?" suggested Di Di, her hand itching either for a drum stick or a pompom. "Dudes!" shouted Billy. "The judges are here."

"Where's Pary?" asked Frank. "Shouldn't Mr. Newduhl be here?" queried Di Di. "Hey look." said Billy as he noticed a handwritten sign on the wall above the light switch near the front of the classroom. It read "When the judges begin their tasting, please turn on the switch." Frank flipped the switch. They heard a soft whirring noise and then Pary Newdul's voice filled the room. Behind the flour and sugar and baking soda canisters, on the counter in the front of the classroom, an old fashioned reel to reel tape recorder was playing a recorded message. "Thank you honored Cordon Bleu Judges" Pary's recorded message began. "Sorry I could not be there this evening. At the last moment a very personal emergency called me away. I hope you enjoy the meal I laid out for you. Bon Appetite! And please remember—I gave it my all."

The judges smacked their lips, helped themselves to seconds and thirds, and then took a quick but almost unnecessary vote and awarded Pary's Special Delights: Cooking Academy the Cordon Bleu Gold Medal Ribbon for the Best Cooking School! They placed the Gold Ribbon on Pary's front counter as they filed out of the room. They wondered out loud about his tasty recipes and the meal's full-bodied flavor.

Di Di and Frank and Billy took it upon themselves to lock up as they were leaving. Billy picked up the Gold Ribbon and studied it for a moment "Dude," he said as he placed the ribbon on the top of the sugar canister. They slammed the door on their way out to make sure it was locked. The small jolt this sent through the building caused the ribbon to slide off the sugar canister and land in between the reels of the tape recorder behind it. Likewise the old wiring in this section of the building also reacted to the jolt with what was probably a short in the wires as Pary's tape recorder suddenly switched on, then paused, then back on. Pary's voice could be heard throughout the room, saying over and over again, faster and faster "I gave it my all...I gave it my all...Igaveitmyall" And then with a shorted out switch, the old tape recorder went into overdrive, caught the ribbon between the whirling reels, and within seconds, the whole thing went up in smoke.

Spider Silk is Stronger Than Steel

Anthony Russell White

I read yesterday in a magazine.
You don't think of that
smashing the well-crafted web
easily,
a brush of your hand,
Superman.
The glistening fat spider
trying to escape
must be killed.
She only knows how to create
spiders
and silk.
What could you create
in a garden
at sunrise?

Alpha Male
Marianne Wolf

Clark Kent flinched and clutched the sheet tight to his chest at the sound of the ring tone. His eyes darkened. He pulled at his tussled hair and, in that moment before focusing his sight toward the digital clock on the nightstand, dragged his hands across his own face feeling the beads of sweat. Clark sat up at the continuous ring, and cursed at his blurred vision. He felt around for his glasses. The ringing seemed louder to him now. Clark scrambled out of bed to grab his Blackberry.

"Clark? Clark, wake up, it's Dave." The voice was calm yet forceful.

"Dave?" Startled, Clark's eyes adjusted to the darkness. He made it to the bathroom in time to see his own outline, slumped with weariness in the reflection of the bathroom mirror.

"Clark? What are you doing? It's time to get down here and sort out these motions with Michael."

"I was trying to get some....sleep." Clark's voice was worn out.

"What's wrong?" he asked skeptically. "You know, we've 108 motions up tomorrow at 10 A.M."

"Yes," Clark's voice sank, "I know."

"Well, you're scaring us. You've been acting a lot like Superman lately. Listen to me Clark, the staff is concerned. They're betting you probably haven't even stopped to eat something today."

"You should be scared." Clark began to pace the floor. "The world is spinning out of control." He felt for the back of his neck, which was suddenly throbbing. "Dave, I want the world to be a safer place. I *must* make the earth a safer place."

"Yes, but Clark, this is too much. You can't single-handedly go before the judges with this massive workload!"

"Yes, *yes* Dave. I know you're right." He let out a pensive sigh. "It's time for *this* Superman to shower and shave. Give me half an hour and I'll meet you and Michael in the hotel's restaurant." He clicked off the phone.

Clark's eyes focused on his face in the mirror. His heart pounded with the heaviness of the task before him. Overcome with helplessness, Clark reached to turn the faucet on and step into the shower. Before he could go any further, Clark heard the bedroom voice of Lois Lane run through his mind. "I have faith in you, Clark. Take care of yourself. You don't have to prove to me or anyone that you're Superman all the time." At the memory of her Clark sunk down on the edge of his big, empty, king-size bed.

In the silence of the moment Clark felt weighed down and alone. Then he remembered the cautionary advice; words from his long-ago mentor: "You are here for a reason."

⊢─┬─┴─┬─┤

Twenty-five years have passed since Clark revealed his secret identity to me. I'm Lois, the woman in the prose you've just read. It honestly never occurred to me when we first met that Clark could be Superman. Do you know how difficult it had been to keep his secret? I'm a writer who needs to tell stories, name names, and let the cat out of the bag. It's been this wicked economy that has set in motion Clark's necessity to switch careers in mid-life and my necessity to write short stories about Clark and his new career. Who would have ever imaged Clark Kent in a mid-life crisis?

When the *Daily Planet* recently filed for bankruptcy it was just one more footnote to the 15,586 jobs eliminated in the newspaper industry. Clark saw the need to retool his career. When the layoffs included yet another 2,500 in just the first two months of the new year, I turned the focus of my writing from reporter to romance, pulp fiction, and science fiction stories.

I remember Clark's first day on the job after graduating from the local university. That was the morning we first met. I was young, beautiful, and a talented writer full of confidence. When he walked into the press room I melted. By deadline, I was smitten, though I would never, ever admit that to Clark, even today. Rather, I appeared cool towards this new man in the pressroom as we were, after all, competitors hunting down the same stories.

Clark had adopted a largely passive and introverted personality, applying conservative Midwestern mannerisms, that higher-than-average pitched voice, and a slight slouch. These traits stretched into Clark's wardrobe, which almost always consisted of soft-colored business suits, red neckties, his signature black-rimmed glasses, combed-back hair and, occasionally, a hat.

In the beginning of his newspaper career everything about Kent was staged for the benefit of *that* alternate identity—he worked as a reporter to receive late-breaking news before the general public (this practice hit the fan with the development of notebook size computers, Blackberries, and Garmins providing affordable navigation to the masses.)

Clark was always running off. Being a reporter at the *Planet*, "that great metropolitan newspaper," allowed him to keep track of ongoing events where he might be of help. Working largely on his own, Clark could easily keep his alter identity a secret. His job provided a reason for being at crime scenes, and as long as he made his deadlines, Clark wasn't too strictly accountable to Perry White, our aggressive editor. But today, in his new career, that Blackberry on his hip rings, vibrates, and sings to him 24-7.

Early on, Clark felt deep personal fulfillment in an intellectual field where his extraordinary abilities gave him no unfair advantage— other than his typing speed on an Underwood typewriter.

Although Kent was often described as "mild-mannered," I know first-hand he could be very assertive, often giving orders to people and taking command of situations without fear of risks. Clark emerged as a central voice in the ongoing debate about city contracts. There had been a heated press conference at Metropolis City Hall where he'd angered the mayor by pursuing allegations of a contractor's mismanagement of the Maxwell Street Market; afterward, I overheard the mayor's press secretary say, "Mr. Kent, you seem to extricate yourself from predicaments by unusual methods which invariably turn out to be legally sound."

"Mild-mannered" doesn't fully evoke what has been and remains Clark's secret passion. Did you know his favorite movie has always been *To Kill a Mockingbird*? His favorite football team: the Metropolis Sharks. His favorite actor has always been Raymond Burr as Perry Mason and only I know Clark secretly had a crush on Perry's secretary, Della Street.

When the economy thrust Clark into the public eye as a super-bulldog litigator, I shouldn't have been surprised by what happened next. He appeared on all of the New York morning news shows; then made an appearance on Larry King Live, followed by a segment with Greta Van Susteren. His defense in dozens of complex class-action cases rocked not just the tall, iron gates of mega-businesses from coast to coast but New York's financial circles as well. It turned Clark into a bit of a reluctant celebrity—the object of friendly ribbing from his colleagues in their newly expanded offices just down the block from Fifth Street and Concord Lane. Even his old fraternity brothers, who used to tip their beer mugs to him when his investigative reporting blew the whistle on City Hall corruption, now joke about his new status. Will he star opposite Glen Close on the hit cable TV series,

Damages? They really let him have it when he appeared on the red carpet at the *Vanity Fair* Oscar party.

"Yes," he'd confided to me with an easy chuckle when a recent conversation turned to *Hollywood*, "it's a little silly. But if you think my appearance on *Damages* would be crazy," he said, "look at the national news."

As for whether Superman the lawyer acting as a TV attorney would trivialize law and turn the centuries-old profession into a farce, "a little bit of fun on television," he said, "is not going to hurt law."

Finally Clark just had to step away from his fascination with the celebrity spotlight to get his life back in order. And keep things on a steady keel with me, the love of his life time.

Though our lifestyles merged perfectly in the beginning, I knew marriage to a super-hero/reporter would be tough. But marriage to a super-hero/attorney in mid-life crisis has been all but impossible. All the attention his cases now generate has turned him into the undisputed champion in the ruthless, back-stabbing world of high-stakes litigators; and a billionaire alpha male changing the colors in his wardrobe. His eyeglasses, now called "transitional lenses," have a no-line bifocal. Even his voice has noticeably deepened. And that slight slouch—gone for good.

166

Clark has had to learn to put much of his own past behind him. This country's economic decline has forced the man of steel to steel his resolve, fight in a new way for someone or something he wanted. He saw his journalist role as an extension of Superman's duties, bringing truth to the forefront and fighting for the little man. Somehow he's convinced this career as a practicing attorney allows him the same responsibilities!

Why didn't I see this coming?

He knows I love him deeply. Still, there are many things that stand in our way that never mattered much before this economic spin. Not just the money thing, the *endless* acquisition of every color Maserati and Ferrari for my man of speed; or the traveling, God knows Clark has *always* been a universal traveler. Lately though, I know Clark has detected something in me. I'm restless. Maybe it's wanting to finally be out-in-the-open after secretly being tied to a man with such an intriguing job. Being Superman *is*, after all, a *job*. It was and is the man who is Clark that I fell in love with. It was a roll of the dice, our love affair. Neither of us knew how things might work out between a super hero and a writer. It's a case that could cost him far more than he's bargained for.

The jury is still out.

Lost in the Bermuda Triangle
Paula Anne Yup

for Jonah

I remember talking to you once
at a clothes exchange held at your place,
how I buy dresses, pants, skirts and blouses
with a whirlwind passion
because as a child I lived on cast-offs
and now I want pretty things,
lots of lots of pretty dresses.
Sometimes, the desire can kill,
the wanting hurts so bad.

So were you right or wrong
to sail off towards Bermuda,
your boat overloaded with too many things?
Nowadays, when I remember you
I remind myself
that we make our own choices
and live our own lives.
But is it this: that the ocean is blue,
very blue
and the fishes,
aren't they pretty creature?
So wear the ocean, I say,
because I can't change the facts.

Tokyo Taxi
Paula Anne Yup

In Shibuya I bought lingerie,
a bra and a slip,
walking Tokyo streets.
Then, as if on a dare,
I walked into the path of a moving car.
When the taxi drive put on his breaks,
honked his horn,
the car skimmed so close
it kissed my dress.
I laughed because he missed.
The next day I flew from Narita,
waving good-bye to my Tokyo lover,
and landed in LA.

goran coban salon

936 W. Diversey Pky, 2nd Floor, Chicago IL 60614
773-248-0077
gorancoban.com / goran@gorancoban.com

"Beauty will change the world…"

Goran Cobanovoski

"Creating Beauty with Healing Hands"

Chicago's Andersonville Neighborhood

Marilyn L. Fumagalli, CMT, LMT
Member AMTA
Belavi Facelift Massage Specialist
MaLoo Botanicals

773-965-0972 or 773-279-0972
fumagalli@ameritech.netwww.belavi.com

About TallGrass Writers Guild

TallGrass Writers Guild is open to all who write seriously at any level. The Guild supports members by providing performance and publication opportunities via its multi-page, bi-monthly newsletter, open mics, formal readings, annual anthologies, and the TallGrass Writers Guild Performance Ensemble programs.

In affiliation with Outrider Press, TallGrass produces its annual "Black-and-White" anthologies, the results of international calls for themed contest entries. Cash prizes and certificates awarded result from the decisions of independent judges.

The Guild is a rarity among arts organizations in that it has been and remains largely self-sufficient despite the challenges facing non-profit arts organizations. For more information on TallGrass Writers Guild membership and programs, call 219-322-7270 or toll-free at 1-866-510-6735. Email tallgrassguild@sbcglobal.net .

About the Judge

Diane ("Diva Di") Williams, author of *Performing Seals*, is a prize-winning poet and essayist who has a novel in progress. A graduate of Chicago's Columbia College, "Judge Diva" was awarded a literary fellowship that took her to Ireland for extensive study. She lives and writes in Chicago, and teaches at Kendall College.

About the Editor

Whitney Scott plays many roles in Chicago's literary scene. She is an author, editor, book designer and reviewer whose poetry, fiction and creative nonfiction have been published internationally, earning her listings in *Contemporary Authors* and *Directory of American Poets and Fiction Writers.*

A member of the Society of Midland Authors, she performs her work at colleges, universities, arts festivals and literary venues throughout the Chicago area and has been featured as guest author in the Illinois Authors Series at Chicago's Harold Washington Library. Scott regularly reviews books for the American Library Association's *Booklist* magazine.

___ **Fearsome Fascinations** –$21.00   _____

Writings on bad boys, vamps, werewolves, forbidden fruits of all kind

___ **Wild Things — Domestic & Otherwise** –$21.00   _____

Writings on bats, rivers...children running wild...

___ **A Walk Through My Garden**–$21.00   _____

Writings on crocuses, composting, digital gardens and more

___ **Vacations: the Good, the Bad & the Ugly** – $20.00   _____

Writings on respites from stolen moments to Roman holidays

___ **Falling in Love Again** – $20.00   _____

Writings on revisiting romance, beloved locales and more

___ **Family Gatherings** – $20.00   _____

Writings on families

___ **Take Two — They're Small** – $20.00   _____

Writings on food

___ **A Kiss Is Still A Kiss** – $19.00   _____

Writings on romantic love

___ **Earth Beneath, Sky Beyond** – $19.00   _____

An anthology on nature and our planet

___ **Feathers, Fins & Fur** – $18.00   _____

Writings on animals

___ **Freedom's Just Another Word** – $17.00   _____

Poetry, fiction and essay on freedom

___ **Alternatives: Roads Less Travelled** – $17.00   _____

Writings on counter-culture lifestyles

___ **Prairie Hearts** – $17.00   _____

Short fiction and poetry on the Heartland

___ **Dancing to the End of the Shining Bar** – $11.95   _____

A novel of love and courage

Add s/h charges:
$3.95 for 1 book...$6.95 for 2 books...
$2.25 each additional book

Send Check or $ Order to:
Outrider Press, Inc.   Total =========
2036 North Winds Drive
Dyer, IN 46311